5 WAYS to SAVE THE PLANET
(in your spare time)

Gregory J. Schwartz
California State University

Taro Patch Small Press
Hanalei   Los Angeles

This book is dedicated to:

the great geographer, and my friend,
Yi-Fu Tuan, in whose midst
my ideas flourished.

Printed On

ISBN # 978-0-9788840-4-8
SAN # 851-8718

Taro Patch Small Press
San Clemente, CA 92672

BISAC Subject Headings:

NAT011000   NATURE / Environmental Conservation & Protection
POL023000   POLITICAL SCIENCE / Economic Conditions
EDU015000   EDUCATION / Higher

www.gregoryjschwartz.com

Contents

THE BIG PICTURE

Introduction – A Moment of Clarity   1

Collective Global Awareness   9

Damsel in Distress (Global Warming)   16

PROBLEMS

Myopia, Indulgence, and Desperation   28

Human Traffic   39

Our Exploding Population   52

The So-Called "Drug War"   62

Dependence on Oil   73

SOLUTIONS

(photos)   90

A Rising Tide Lifts All Boats   85

Beacon of Light   93

5 Ways to Save the Planet:

1. Convert to Solar   97

2. Eat Organic   109

3. Give (Benevolent Individuals)   123

           (Benevolent Organizations)   134

4. Uplift Women   144

5. Make Your Household Efficient   159

CONCLUSION

The Gift of Tragedy   180

Practical Suggestions for Saving the Planet   194

Citations and Bibliography   201

Adventure Travel Stories   1, 16, 22, 28, 33, 42, 50
                          62, 73, 90, 93, 110, 119, 172

Introduction

Traveling through Malaysia in the late 1990s, I was eager to stretch my legs when the bus finally pulled into a rest stop at the crest of a small hill. Stepping outside into the humid tropical air, I heard myself gasp as I saw miles of ancient rainforest stretched out in front of me as far as the eye could see.

The forest was painted a rich, dark green and buzzing with the sounds of Mother Nature's life force. It felt like I was standing in the thriving, pulsing center of the entire natural world. I had finally found what I had been searching for: nature in its purest and richest form. And it was deeply fulfilling. This moment came in stark contrast to the preceding few days of the journey where I had seen large sections of deforested and scorched land being readied for plantations and development. Within the previous month, I had passed through giant shanty towns that surrounded the region's biggest cities where millions of people lived in squalor.

It was then that it hit me: no matter who we are or

where we live, the world's problems are now at our doorstep. Deforestation doesn't just affect Thailand or Brazil – it is destroying the lungs of the entire planet. An economic downturn in Japan or debt defaults in Africa immediately affect global markets and national budgets. Blissful ignorance of other nations and of our environment is no longer an option. Yet at some point in our routine of morning lattes and nightly TiVo, many of us have somehow been lulled to sleep; meanwhile our beautiful planet is slipping away. We have allowed ourselves to be distanced from nature, believing that we are apart from the natural world rather than a living part of it. And all of us at times acquiesce to the illusion that society is a competition between "us" and "them," which allows us to support policies that dehumanize and mistreat our neighbors. Standing in the Malaysian rainforest, in that moment of clarity, I wanted to yell so loud that the entire world would wake up … and change.

For two decades I journeyed through Africa, Central America, Europe, South America, the Middle East, and Southeast Asia, and I witnessed much of the world's beauty and dynamism: an expanding environmental and human rights consciousness, the globalization of culture and communication, a growing tide of international philanthropy and altruism, and a move toward sustainable energy and agriculture. Yet at the same time I gradually grew overwhelmed at the scale of human suffering and environmental harm that is going on right now on our planet: rapid deforestation and wars over resources, global warming, an international sex and drug trade, rampant starvation, war and terrorism, and an exploding population.

Understanding the causes of this degradation and suffering quickly became the focus of my academic research, my travel, and my writing and teaching. After several years, I came to comprehend something amazing about the world's plight: the solutions to our biggest problems already exist, and they have for quite some time. For instance, we have enough food for everyone on the planet, but we throw away 16 million tons of food annually in the U.S. alone, and grain surpluses rot in the Western world while entire nations suffer through famine. We eat so much in the wealthy nations that it is killing us, while 15,000 people starve to death every day elsewhere.

Likewise, huge solar power plants were fully operational 100 years ago, and more electric cars were on American roads in 1900 than gas-powered ones. The harmful climate change, pollution, loss of life, and skyrocketing financial cost of excessive dependence on fossil fuels was never necessary, and even less so now. So why do so many people continue to starve, and why do we insist on our unnecessary addiction to fossil fuels?

If we just passed out mosquito nets, as UNICEF and others now do, two million African children would not die from malaria each year. The same is true of inexpensive AIDS drugs. Moreover, some focus on demonizing the Middle East and cultivating a lifestyle of fear of terrorism, never considering that by invading Iraq and Afghanistan and killing hundreds of thousands of their soldiers and citizens in our quest for oil, we (Western nations) are stoking the very fire that burns us.

Most of the solutions to our most critical problems are reasonable, simple, and they are already here. They have been within our grasp for many decades. We have the manpower, the technology, and the logical solutions to our problems. So our main limitations are not tangible, they are intangible. What hinders us is not what we have, but what we think and believe.

A few core beliefs about the world and how the world works form the foundation for our decisions as individuals. What each of us thinks about love, money, or God, for instance, has a significant and guiding influence on our choices and actions in those specific parts of our lives. Our deepest beliefs profoundly help or hinder us, yet most of us are not even conscious of them.

One powerful but also limiting belief that has

guided civilization for millennia is this: advancement is achieved through conquest. Civilizations have expanded and "progressed" through conquering others militarily and economically. This has been true with cultures from the Egyptians, Aztecs, and Romans to the Mongols, Turks, European colonizers, and modern day super-powers. This allowed some societies to grow, acquire wealth and resources, and develop technologically and culturally. Under this belief, advancement has indeed occurred, yet at great toll to those who were conquered. It has left a wake of destruction and has eradicated cultures, histories, human life, resources, and good will between societies. On some levels, the belief that advancement is achieved through conquest benefitted the world for many centuries, but it appears that it no longer serves us.

What if we began to make a different assumption -- that advancement and abundance is achieved through cooperation and union? The world would change profoundly and rapidly. Copious evidence of the truth of this divine idea is presented herein, and in fact, only our staunch limiting belief in the opposite has shrouded the beauty and simplicity of this mutual uplifting for millennia. This concept is developed further in the chapter entitled "A Rising Tide Lifts All Boats."

A second shift in mindset is the move beyond logic and reason and into compassion. It is often said that what separated modern man from the animal kingdom, and even from his prehistoric ancestors, was his ability to use logic and reason rather than just brute strength or animal instincts. In the 21st century, another leap in consciousness is called for. Now what separates those who are healing the planet from those who continue to ignore and damage it is the ability to empathically feel the needs and struggles of others. This empathy is sourced in the heart and not in the mind. Ghandi, Martin Luther King, Jr., and John Muir embodied this empathy. Those who feel the pain of their neighbors and sense the needs of the planet display compassion, and are often moved to play a part in rectifying these ills. Therefore, in this movement to save the planet, perhaps even more important than changing our minds is changing our hearts.

Third, what we define as wealth must center less on money and traditional economics and more on the true, irreplaceable gifts of this life: our physical health, the beauty and resources of the natural world, and our sacred relationships with those we love and with our fellow man. If we continue to focus on money at the expense of the environment and of our neighbor, then our water, air, and soil will be so degraded that our Earth will become unlivable and the foundation of our lives here will disintegrate. When we make choices that heal our environment, cultivate our physical health, and end needless suffering, then we will realize that true wealth is everywhere and there is plenty to go around.

A fourth limiting belief, centered in the Western (non-Asian) part of the world, is simply the placing of heavy emphasis on individual responsibility rather than collective responsibility (1). Individualism and self-sufficiency are certainly virtues -- central tenets of the Republican political philosophy in the United States, in fact. They were essential to the successful development and growth of the European and American societies. Yet when magnified by vaulted success and two centuries of social evolution, this approach has placed 80 percent of the world's wealth in the hands of only 10 percent of its people, even within wealthy Western countries. Therefore, this approach does not serve society or benefit us as it once did. Shifting from a self-centered world view to a global consciousness is now called for in order for society to move forward. It undergirds the realization that, in fact, we are all one.

Fifth and finally, as Al Gore suggests in "An Inconvenient Truth," we must resist the temptation, when first encountering an imposing challenge, to jump from ignorance to overwhelmed despair. Neither ignorance nor despair produce good or generate change. It is so very critical that we learn to inhabit that precious middle ground where we seek awareness of the world's problems, yet do not become overwhelmed or simply give up when we comprehend their extent. Rather, we can acknowledge these problems, accept our partial role in causing them, then commit to taking even the smallest steps toward solving them. This is conveyed by a popular Kenyan phrase "Kidogo Kidogo" (take it little by little). No single one of us has to save the world on his own. Indeed, no individual can. We simply are called to take notice and play a tiny part in the healing.

At countless times in history, outdated beliefs needed to be replaced by progressive, new ideas in order for the world to move forward. What shape would the Western world be in if the Greeks had not stepped past dictatorship and developed democracy? How did countless countries operate before women could legally vote? And who can imagine that fifty years ago the United States had yet to pass the Civil Rights Act? These shifts in beliefs were necessary and sweeping and they brought about changes without which our world is difficult to imagine.

Many of the beliefs that no longer serve or benefit us are based in fear. Fear leads to aggression and separation, which divulges an over-emphasis on male "yang" energy, and not enough female "yin" energy. Masculine energy produces competition, action, and decisiveness, which is beneficial and prodigious. Yet an overly male-centered approach can produce war and vast imbalances, which is what we are experiencing on the planet today. These conflicts, in turn, lead to more fear, and the cycle perpetuates.

Beliefs that generate connections and abundance are based, at their root, in love. They are focused on communication, mutual awareness and giving, which are associated with the female approach yet at the core of all human beings. This approach cultivates healthy relationships, both personal and political, and condones the circulation and flow of ideas, goods, and people. It is founded on an awareness of the Earth and of our fellow human, and an acknowledged responsibility for them. The planet, like each person, is a balance of feminine and masculine energy: a whole with two essential parts. Right now, a quelling of excessive masculine energy along with a cultivation of the female yin energy and mindset is required to bring the planet, along with many of us, into balance.

Along with this shift in some of our core beliefs, there are critical tangible steps that need to be taken in order to transform the world into a better place. In the following chapters, I highlight five specific actions — 5 Ways to Save the Planet — that have global-scale impacts as well as positive ripple effects that reverberate through many layers of society. These five ways are the solutions which have already existed for decades yet simply await full implementation. Organic farming, for example, improves soil quality, which keeps our farms healthy and productive long into the future. Organic food also helps to decrease obesity and several kinds of cancer, which lessens health care costs. Also, converting to renewables like solar and wind power dramatically lessens CO_2 production, decreases our need for wars overseas, and saves hundreds of billions of dollars on extracting, transporting, and cleaning up fossil fuels.

This book details how in order to solve the world's problems, wealthy, developed nations have roles to play with specific pursuant actions, as do poorer, developing nations. Consumption and apathy are at the root of our problems in the developed world, while isolation and survival by any means necessary are leading to unwise choices in the developing world.

In order for this change in beliefs and actions to congeal, we must shift our regular mode of operating. The transformation has already begun to emerge and it is the natural course of events: we as a planet returning to harmony and returning to our nature as an interconnected, inter-loving whole. Yet still, this shift is in our hands and we must choose it in order for it to come to fruition. It is up to those who are aware and those who have the power to help. And so then, by that definition, it is up to you.

Collective Global Awareness

"Awareness is the best friend of the environment and the common good and it is the greatest enemy of avarice, abuse, and injustice."

- Joy Palmer, February 2003

At 8:30p.m. on March 27, 2010, a large percentage of people on planet Earth did a powerful yet simple collective act; they turned off the lights. During "Earth Hour," as it was called, hundreds of millions of people in thousands of cities turned off their lights for exactly one hour as a symbolic and tangible acknowledgement of the need to reduce global carbon emissions. That one rolling blackout around the globe saved the equivalent of millions of pounds of CO_2 from being released into our air.

Our awareness of each other and of the issues that we face as a planet, combined with our ability to simply communicate with each other, can create astonishing results in a very short amount of time. A collective awareness – the basic realization that we are all a part of one living, whole entity – is one of the most important shifts in consciousness that is happening on our planet right now.

We are becoming more aware of each other and of what is going on with nature, society, the global economy, wars both large and small, and injustices across the globe. This is critical because malice and oppression cease to have power in the light of awareness. In darkness, iniquity and conflict fester and grow much like bacteria grows in a dark, cold cellar or disease flourishes in the body of an unexamined psyche and ignored soul. Awareness is the beginning of solutions, the remedy to darkness, and it is critical to our healing and evolution as a planet. All we must do is expose injustice by shifting our gaze upon it, and the healing and transformation can rush in. All we have to do, literally, is communicate with each other, interact with each other, and become aware of each other. In this way, the evils in the world can be exposed and rectified. A festering wound needs to be rinsed and cleansed. Massive personal and national debts need to be acknowledged and dealt with. And social and environmental abuses need to be brought to the light of day.

Our expanded awareness and connectedness is growing through several clear mechanisms: improved transportation, improved communication, an expansion of the omnipresence of news media, and the globalization of culture. For nearly two centuries, trains and ocean liners were the only option for transporting people and goods. Now, jet air travel allows for the meshing of ideas, cultural cross-pollination, and a unification of the globe in an immediate physical and visceral sense. During part of a whirlwind trip in 1999, my family and I had breakfast in Europe, lunch in Asia, and dinner in Africa, all in the same day! That was not possible several decades ago.

Improved communication, principally through a proliferation of cell phones and access to the Internet, has also radically changed how and how much information flows. In Western and industrialized countries, these technologies are very prevalent, yet they have a presence in essentially every global region. In 2002, there were 298 million cell phone users in the European Union, which is 79% of the population. In some locations, such as Luxembourg, there are more cell phones than people (1). Currently, about 150 million people in Europe use the Internet, which is one-third of the total populace, while 90% of schools in the region have an Internet connection. Moreover, worldwide 500 million people now have an account on Facebook. Not surprisingly, three of the most reported uses of the Internet are for e-mail, access to news, and meeting new people or socializing. All of these activities foster an awareness of our fellow man, especially for those who are in geographically isolated regions.

The Internet also fosters new non-territorial communities, which shatter spatial considerations of a community or nation. It allows for the safe, constant, and mass-scale human interaction that form part of the foundation of a global consciousness. Yet taken to an extreme, this feeling of belonging to a cyber community can be disorienting.

"In an age where people have more opportunity to be interconnected across space and time through technologically-aided communication than during any other period in history, the (post) modern individual in contemporary Western society is paradoxically feeling increasingly isolated. New ways to understand and experience meaningful togetherness are being sought" (2).

This feeling of isolation brought on by techno-proliferation, however, can be cited as the source of another positive trend on the globe, which is a reconnection with the local. This "tribalism," and deliberate return to local social, economic, and cultural entities is paralleled by the huge and recent rise in localized energy and food production. Solar energy is the fastest-growing energy source on Earth, due in large part to the fact that it can be generated locally and on a small scale without costly infrastructure. Organic farming, largely cultivated for local consumption, is also expanding very rapidly in the United States and Europe, as well as in much of the third world as a response to the chemical-intensive "green revolution" in agribusiness.

Another facet of our unification as a planet is the globalization of culture, which has become synonymous with the Americanization of culture. For better or worse, the United States dominates most media. American movies are seen in almost every country on Earth, and they often take in more money and usurp more screens in foreign countries than movies produced in that home country. Even in epicurean cultural centers like France, American blockbusters are shown in the majority of theatres. American TV programs are no different. 75% of all purchased non-domestic TV programming in the world is from the U.S. That is, if a country buys television programming from another country, three-fourths of the time it is from the U.S. (3). Moreover, 18 of the all-time 25 best-selling musical artists are American, including (in U.S. sales alone) Garth Brooks with 104 million album sales, Elvis Presley with 86 million, Madonna with 59 million, and Michael Jackson with 58 million (4).

The cultural phenomenon of MTV has, in the words of *Jihad vs. McWorld* author Benjamin Barber, become the true Trojan horse of American culture in foreign societies. Ten years after its inception in the late 1980s, MTV was being broadcast to 201 million households in 77 countries. By 1995 the vast majority of nations in the world, barring a smattering of land-locked developing world nations, had MTV or a similar domestic reproduction of it (5).

The satellite dish is also an important technology in this trend. American television can now find its way into foreign cultures – even isolated, traditional, or authoritarian ones. Radio waves go over walls and through centuries-old traditions, right into the living rooms of citizens (6). Like solar energy collectors, satellite dishes do not require expensive ground line infrastructure. They are independent, powerful, and localized. Star TV, a satellite network owned by Rupert

Murdoch, who also owns all FOX networks, is shown to 300 million viewers in Asia. The "Eutelsat" satellite system sends programming to Europe, the Middle East, and North Africa into 52.6 million homes (7). Moreover, author Lane Crothers states that:

"As satellite systems proliferate, they need to fill the immense bandwidth on which they broadcast. Ready-made and already proven popular (on movie screens), American programming provides easy filler. Under such circumstances it is reasonable to expect American television programming to proliferate globally in coming years" (8).

That the substance of American society has come to infiltrate the globe is well established. Traditional cultures are bending and yielding to its momentum, power, and likeability. Yet conversely, the source of this culture – America itself – is a cultural amalgam from around the world. We are a microcosm of the world. Except for the Native Americans, everyone in the U.S. is a fairly recent immigrant, the vast majority of us being here for less than six generations. Hence, we are all "from another country." And so American culture is necessarily a fresh and multi-influenced, dynamic cultural package that is being broadcast to the world through various media. In this way, we are globally united under a universalizing cultural essence which is being beamed out into the world, and that essence is a blend, and an almost (though not quite) democratic representation of the societies which are receiving it.

The last development or entity which is fuel for the augmenting knowledge of the world and of one's neighbors is the omnipresence of the media. Ted Turner's gutsy venture to provide the first twenty-four hour news channel on CNN proved a huge success and changed the role and scope of news media forever. It modified how governments and citizenry interact. It empowered citizens by giving them a voice and a window to the world, while simultaneously making governments accountable for their actions and policies. The recent expansion of news media presence and programming, perhaps more than any other modern entity, has shed a light of awareness across the Earth. The prevalence and nature of genocide, military action, and human rights abuses in particular, were immediately affected. This new-found power of the media to effect real change and influence popular knowledge to such a degree has also come with responsibility.

News networks are in a privileged position to help guide public awareness and shape our knowledge of the world. Their shaping of statistics, images, and the perception of events has enormous power to reconcile, heal, and ameliorate political, environmental, and social injustices. A shift from sensationalism – the pursuit of blood, conflict, and shocking footage at any cost – toward a responsible investigation and delivery of the core events, with the intent to actually help and not just observe, is crucial. There is already evidence of this transformation in both news and other media forms as these groups are accepting their new role with a willing, albeit often profit-driven, air of social responsibility.

CBS producer Mark Johnson pulled a violent criminal series called "Falcone" in the months following the Columbine school bloodshed. MTV banned guns in videos some years ago, and in 1998 began a movement against violence recognizable by the slogan "Take a Stand Against Violence." And as a result, violence actually shows signs of losing its public cachet. "The public, through ticket sales, showed it is no longer interested in that," remarked the president of Lion Gate Films, Peter Strauss. Television shows that have recently been described as dealing positively with trauma, violence, and displaying realistic pathways to healing are: Boston Public, House, Scrubs, 7th Heaven, Beverly Hills 90210, and Buffy the Vampire Slayer (9).

The lunar landing of July 1969 was also brought to

the world through the medium of television. From the moon's surface, one particular photograph was taken which came to be called "Earth rise." That picture quickly became the world's most published photograph. Its prevalence alone seems to have changed how we view our Earth, because less than a year later, the globe's modern environmental movement was begun (10).

The ability of increased communication, transportation, globalization of culture, and media exposure to spread awareness – and hence light – into every corner of the globe is immense indeed. Amidst this expanding interconnectivity, there is already evidence of a collaborative responsibility among those who have the power to effect change. The television and movie industries, along with news networks, are finding that highlighting the positive and noble aspects of people and events is beneficial both for political and social coherence as well as for ratings and sales. This so-called "Oprah Winfrey Factor" of focusing on and cultivating the good in people and institutions is simple, yet nothing less than transformative to society. Becoming aware of iniquity and what's "wrong" with our planet and letting it heal, together with a nascent focus on what is "right" and inspiring in the world constitutes perhaps the most beneficial reconciliation of our conscious power to better the world in our collective history.

When the light of awareness and attention on the positive meets the darkness of mistreatment and injustice, there is no contest. The battle is already won. Because, as paraphrased from a comment made by Albert Einstein in response to a professor's question in college, "There is no true darkness, only the temporary and perceived absence of light."

Damsel in Distress

Global Warming has our Mother Earth in Dire Straits

"I really feel that nature is trying so hard to compensate for man's mismanagement of the planet. The planet is sick – like a fever. If we don't fix it now, it's at the point of no return... The time has come. This is it. People are always saying 'Oh, they'll take care of it, the government will, they will,' .... They Who? It starts with us. It's us, or else it'll never be done."

- Michael Jackson, King of Pop, philanthropist, and environmentalist, in 2009 documentary "This is it."

Standing at around 8,000 feet in the Swiss Alps and gazing at the majestic peak of the Matterhorn, it didn't make sense to me that the massive glacier we were standing on hadn't melted more by this late in July. "It melts a lot in the summer but then expands in the winter," said our college-aged guide from the nearby town of Zermatt, "but it is smaller now than it was when I was a boy. It shrinks more every year." The year was 1990 and "global warming" wasn't a common term yet, but the experience caught my interest.

Six years later, I found myself in East Africa speaking to villagers and international aid workers from Arusha,

Tanzania near the base of Mount Kilimanjaro. "The ice is disappearing," was the conclusion of one villager and itinerant climbing guide. He was correct, because today, sadly, only specks of Kilimanjaro's beautiful glaciers remain, and within a decade they will be completely gone. The story was the same when I climbed to 16,500 feet in the Andes Mountains of Chile during that same year, and a train ride in 1994 through the barren landscape of Glacier National Park in Montana now seemed poignantly foretelling.

Global warming is a tangible reality world-wide. It is very simply the most pressing threat to the continuance of life on Earth as we know it. Several issues discussed in the chapters following, such as deforestation, what we eat, and how we use energy, are causes of global warming, so it is a theme that will be touched upon often. The gravity of this issue necessitates its placement at the beginning of this book, as well as at the forefront of more of our everyday conversations.

The fact that the globe is warming up is finally widely accepted, even by most staunch conservatives. The controversy concerning whether the warming is anthropogenic, or human-caused, essentially only exists in popular magazines, websites, and radio and television programs. Among academics and scientists who are published in scientifically refereed journals, there is a virtual consensus that current global warming rates are largely, if not overwhelmingly, caused by carbon dioxide from burning fossil fuels and burning rainforest. In simplest terms, this carbon dioxide in the atmosphere acts like the glass shell of a greenhouse by allowing light and heat to enter, but trapping some of the heat before it escapes. The more carbon dioxide, the more heat that is trapped, and the warmer the planet becomes.

In her recent article in National Geographic magazine entitled "Water is Life," Barbara Kingsolver shares that Earth's average temperature has recently escalated by about 1.5 degrees Farenheit (1). This number may sound insignificant, but if your freezer is set to 31.5 degrees Farenheit and everything is frozen solid, if the temperature is raised to just 33 degrees, suddenly everything melts into liquid. In many regions in the Spring and Fall, temperatures walk that fine line on the freeze/melt point and 1.5 degrees of difference stretched over months is making a world of difference.

Although cooling and warming cycles are normal for the Earth, a human-induced warming has never been witnessed before now, so its effects are quite unpredictable. It took millions of years to store excess carbon in the form of fossil fuels under the ground, yet we are burning and releasing them in their entirety all within a few hundred years. This is returning all of that stored carbon back into the air and hence drastically altering the composition of the Earth's atmosphere. Massive changes are literally afoot and the natural world is changing fast. Global sea level rose about six to eight inches in the 20th century (2), but most conservative gauges estimate that it will rise from two to six feet in the 21st century (3). Many well-established estimates are much higher.

This means that, in coming decades, hundreds of millions of coastal inhabitants will be forced to relocate. Also, warming is destroying countless plant and animal habitats, resulting in rampant species extinctions. The current rate of extinction of birds, mammals, reptiles, and frogs is occurring at 20 to 1000 times the normal "background" rate, depending on the region (4). Animal migration patterns, food supplies, and feeding hierarchies (food webs) are being altered or eliminated, which, combined with pollution and deforestation, is tearing the fundamental fabric of nature. Because of these shifts, in only fifty years, we will be living on a different planet than we are today. In the words of authors William Antholis and Strobe Talbott, "If we do not start the process of mitigating climate change right now, our descendants, however skilled, will not be able to cope with the consequences" (5). In accord with their assessment, I do not jest when I suggest that you go see the rainforest and the planet's glaciers and endangered animals within the next decade or two -- while they still exist.

By way of our massive annual release of carbon into the air, we are recreating conditions that existed on the Earth tens of millions of years ago in the Eocene era. At that time, huge quantities of CO_2 filled our atmosphere, heating the entire planet, melting the poles, and turning Earth into a veritable water world. Plant life began to flourish and consume this copious carbon, especially via algae in the oceans, which led to a gradual decrease in the greenhouse effect and hence a decrease in global temperature over several millennia. When these carbon-rich plants and algae died and fell to the ocean floor, they could not decay and release their carbon content since there was such a dearth of oxygen in that deep ocean environment. Hence, they simply piled up, and over millions of years these carbon-infused plant fossils were transformed into fossil fuels, namely oil and natural gas. Coal is formed in a similar way, but with decaying plants on land and in swamps. When we burn these fossil fuels in order to access their stored life energy, the carbon in them is released back into the atmosphere. Hence, by burning the vast majority of oil and coal reserves on the planet, we are putting millions of years of stored carbon back into the air within a matter of about 200 years. Therefore we are simply re-creating the conditions that previously converted Earth into a water world.

One point that is only beginning to enter energy-use discussions in earnest is that although our oil supply is rapidly drying up, the U.S. alone has a 100 to 250-year supply of coal reserves at current usage rates (6). Burning coal releases significantly more CO_2 than oil per unit of energy produced, along with toxins such as arsenic and mercury, so even as oil reserves slowly recede, long-term pollution from coal still looms large. This is why renewable energies like wind and solar, in particular, are both critical and remarkable. On one hand, they are energy sources that continuously flow and never run out, and on the other hand, they replace coal – the dirtiest fossil fuel – as the principle generator of our electricity. Wind and sun, unlike coal and oil, don't have to be searched for, dug up, transported, refined, or burned, which saves unimaginable amounts of energy. So as we convert to renewables, we replace the most-polluting energy source on the planet with energy sources that produce essentially no pollution at all. That constitutes one of the best environmental and economic boons that the Earth will experience in the next century. Currently renewables produce over 7% of the 100 quadrillion BTU of energy consumed each year in the United States. The majority of that renewable energy is generated from hydroelectric dams. Wind power and solar power combine to satisfy only about 1.5% of the U.S. total energy demand, but that number is growing fast (7).

In 2009, the global population released about 59 trillion pounds of CO_2 into Earth's atmosphere. That's 160 billion pounds released every day (8). The U.S. produces over one-fifth of the globe's CO_2, while only ten countries combine to produce nearly 70% of total global CO_2 emissions (9). The lion's share of CO_2 is released through the burning of fossil fuels. A distant second, producing an estimated 20-25% as much carbon, is forest clearing and burning (10). After that, industrial sources such as the manufacture of fertilizers and chemicals like lime generate a tertiary level of CO_2 emissions.

Of course, skeptics often remark that animals, humans, and plants produce carbon dioxide all the time through respiration, which is a valid point. Yet the total biotic production of CO_2 (from living things and from soil) is easily absorbed by the process of photosynthesis in the world's plants. In fact, plants utilize the CO_2 as fuel to produce both oxygen and sugar, which allows for human life to exist on Earth. When we breathe this oxygen and burn this plant food in the form of simple sugars, we release carbon dioxide again for plants to use, and this so-called "carbon cycle" begins again.

What is throwing off the carbon cycle is the fact that we are digging up and burning fossil fuels, which pumps more CO_2 into the air than the planet's plants can utilize (11). The excess carbon is heating up the planet and acidifying our rain and our oceans. Exacerbating the problem, of course, is that just as we are pumping more and more carbon dioxide into the air, we are cutting down trees which are the only entity that can clean the air by metabolizing the carbon. This is why we are in such a fix. Half of the forests on the planet are already gone and we lose another 50,000 to 100,000 acres per day, depending on which estimates are read. Moreover, only about a fifth of original "old growth" forests remain, principally in Colombia, Venezuela, Suriname, Canada, Alaska, the Russian Taiga, and the Guyanas of South America. For instance, according to the National Park Service, a full 96% of the original old growth redwood forests of the U.S. west coast have already been logged.

These pristine virgin forests have astonishing biodiversity and some of the highest levels of energy and energetic vibration found in the natural world. This elevated vibration could be described as nature's consciousness, the planet's intelligence, or the soul of Mother Nature. An excellent depiction of this beautiful essence is found in the motion picture, Avatar, now the best-selling movie of all time. The movie's "Navi" people are a part of nature, not apart from it, and their synergy with nature allows both their natural world as well as their culture to truly flourish. When we understand these precious ecosystems from this perspective, it is much tougher to scoff at "tree-huggers" and hopefully more difficult to reduce our natural resources to pure economic commodities which are to be harvested, bought and sold as such. In the words of Hilary Benn, U.K. Secretary of State for Environment, Food, and Rural Affairs, "The time has come for us to put sustainable development into action, for the good of our forests, the lives they sustain, the biodiversity they support, and the survival of our planet" (12).

Visiting thirty-nine countries over the past thirty years of my life, I've been privileged to see some of nature's most dramatic and beautiful displays, which has fortified my love of this planet. In Costa Rica, I bathed in lava-heated hot springs with my family as Mount Arenal volcano erupted in full view only a few hundred yards away. In Kenya, I camped on the Serengeti Plain with Masai tribesmen, listening to lions and hyenas howling at night -- then by day witnessing giant herds of grazing elephants and the necks of twenty-foot-tall giraffes reaching up to break the horizon miles away. Free diving off a fishing boat in the Pacific Ocean near the equator, I suddenly found myself surrounded by a menacing school of sharks, each eight to ten feet in length. They took turns swimming toward me, mocking an attack, then darting away at the last moment. After getting over my initial reaction of acute primal fear, I realized that perhaps they just wanted a better look, or that they were just testing me and monitoring my responses. Either way, I suddenly felt relatively safe…. in the middle of a school of sharks!

Off the coast of Vietnam, I gazed down to the ocean floor through fifty feet of the clearest turquoise water I've ever seen, before or since. I've traversed the mountains of northern Thailand on the back of an elephant, navigated its rivers on a bamboo raft, and seen the nutrient-rich waters of the Mekong River fertilize its delta and grow enough rice to feed ten million people. I once ran for miles through thick Central American tropical jungle like an animal, my eyes and ears trained on every incoming sight and sound, only to plunge, breathing heavily and profusely sweating, into the odd silence of an open, barren field which had been recently deforested. I saw the pageantry and demonstrative transformation of the changing seasons in Madison, Wisconsin during my graduate school years – once swimming nearly two miles across Lake Mendota, and then walking the same exact path over the frozen lake in winter. Perhaps as preparation for this range of experience, I spent the first eighteen years of my life in the blissful perpetuity of southern California's unchanging climate: 72 degrees and sunny nearly all year round.

I am truly enchanted by this beautiful planet and all of its natural rhythms. I always felt a kinship with nature as a child, and traveling the world to see its diversity, beauty and dynamism has only enriched that love and appreciation. I have studied Geography for many years and now I teach this subject in college. Geography is the study of how the processes of the Earth affect human beings and how human civilization affects the Earth. Having this background is, no doubt, why I feel so deeply affected by the way that nature is abused and disregarded around the globe out of ignorance and apathy, most often for simple monetary gain.

But thankfully this is changing! Speaking specifically of human-induced global warming, CO_2 production is certainly the crux of the problem, and a shift to renewable energies is the simple and clear solution. In fact, once it truly soaks into our brains how remarkable, simple, and practical solar and wind power are, the change will be very, very rapid. We are so willing to bear the deeply negative social, environmental and economic ramifications of oil and coal use that I truly think it is a challenge for us to imagine that we can have plenty of energy – in fact, infinitely more – yet not incur those same problems. Global warming, acid rain, air pollution, smog in every major global city, trillions in tax dollars spent on war, thousands killed in wars, thousands killed mining coal each year (13), millions of gallons of oil spilled into the ocean every year, billions in tax dollars spent searching for oil, terrorist retaliation for our oil-related military aggression: all of these negatives are a not a part of everyday life, they are a part of oil and coal. This is a fact that purveyors of oil and coal have desperately tried, and largely succeeded, to hide from the world over the past century. The suppression of information, technology and commercial opportunities for renewable energy comprises a hearty sub-plot in 20th century international geopolitics.

Besides shifts in beliefs and awareness, renewable energies are the single most important tangible solution to the planet's current problems. It is elating to encounter a manifestly clear solution to such a pressing problem. Solving disease, starvation, racism, political corruption, and war all involve more complex processes and timelines, though they are certainly also solvable. Yet global CO_2 production can be significantly cut within a decade if we simply choose it and cultivate the shift of jobs from the fossil fuel industries to renewables. Receiving energy at a fraction of the current cost will dramatically ameliorate city, state, and national government budgets across the world.

Another pillar of the solution to global warming is curtailing and eventually ceasing deforestation. Removing trees is in essence the quickest way to kill the planet, so protecting our forests must be of highest priority. This problem isn't easily solved because there are many forces pushing for deforestation and only a few pushing for conservation. Poverty and population pressure are the main causes of the trend, and those are substantial problems in their own right. A few specific causes of deforestation are agriculture, cash crop plantations, selling timber, road building, urbanization and tourism space development, oil prospecting, and clearing space for cattle grazing or for growing crops that will feed cattle. The easiest way for those living in wealthy countries to help stop deforestation is to donate to their favorite environmental NGO, or to one that focuses on deforestation such as the Rainforest Action Network, Environmental Defense Fund, Rainforest Alliance, Amazon Watch, Friends of the Earth, and the Sierra Club. We can also be mindful of buying only from companies whose production processes do not necessitate deforestation.

Rainforest Action Network (RAN) influences many

companies to adopt less environmentally damaging practices. A recent boycott against Burger King pressured the corporation to cancel $35 million in beef contracts in Central America, leading to a slowing of clearing forest for beef production in the region (14). The Friends of the Earth (FOE) "Mahogany is Murder" campaign cut mahogany imports to the UK nearly in half from 1992 to 1996, while RAN's "Teak is Torture" campaign led to boycotts against products produced in Burma (15). Moreover, in mid 2010, Greenpeace won a major victory when Nestle Corporation agreed to significantly diminish its purchase of palm oil from tropical plantations. Palm oil plantations are the number one cause of deforestation in Indonesia, as well as in much of the tropics, so as a Greenpeace member, I was particularly gratified with this major victory.

Legendary performer Michael Jackson's hit "Earth Song" was accompanied by a poignant music video which manifested his open denouncement of global deforestation. In interviews as well, Michael has been very vocal (no pun intended) about his love of the natural world. As heard in his 2009 documentary "This is it," Michael stated:

"I respect the secrets and magic of nature. That's why it makes me so angry when I see that ... every second I hear the size of a football field (of rainforest) is torn down in the Amazon. That kind of stuff really bothers me. That's why I write these kinds of songs... to give some sense of awareness and awakening and hope to people."

J.P. Morgan, Goldman Sachs, Citigroup, and Bank of America all have infused elaborate environmental policies into their regular operating procedures, which is very encouraging. Goldman Sachs was the most recent to do so. Several companies actually purchase large sections of forest in order to ensure that it will not be cut down. Patagonia clothing company is one of them. They recently purchased over 200,000 acres of land in their namesake region of Chile and Argentina. Moreover, one success of the December 2009 Copenhagen environmental summit was the creation of the $3.5 billion REDD fund (reducing emissions from deforestation and forest degradation) which was established by the U.K., Japan, Australia, France, Norway and the U.S. It provides funds to regions threatened by the most rampant deforestation (16).

It is encouraging that on the corporate level and to a smaller extent on the national level, there is action being taken to lessen deforestation. But the response needs to be much bigger and more widespread, so let's not let ourselves off the hook from playing at least a small role in helping! If every American gave one dollar to their favorite environmental organization, then $300,000,000 dollars would suddenly be working to protect the environment the very next day. That is very powerful. Another big way to help is to cut down on the consumption of beef. In other chapters I discuss how cattle grazing and growing crops to feed cattle are responsible for as much as one-third of forest clearing in the Amazon. The other side of the coin is choosing renewable energy. Some companies now install solar panels on your home for no money down, and conscientiously voting on renewable energy proposals and initiatives can have a huge impact as well.

Thomas Jefferson once wrote that "the earth belongs in usufruct (trust) to the living... no generation can contract debts greater than may be paid during the course of its own existence" (17). So whenever you can, take the steps that are manageable to you – conservation, voting, or donating -- that can fight global warming and keep the planet healthy for the next generation.

The Earth provides for us without question or limit and now it needs our love and care in return. I trust that we will give it nothing less than that.

PROBLEMS

Myopia, Indulgence and Desperation

An Overview of the Source of Our Struggles

"Fear is the path to the Dark Side. Fear leads to anger, anger leads to hate, hate leads to suffering."

- Yoda, Star Wars Episode 1

One summer during the late 90s, I found myself traveling alone in East Africa. During a phone call home, I was urged by my mother to be careful because the U.S. State Department's website admonished of a war and political instability in the East African region. I instantly wondered where this war was going on, because there was no evidence of it in Kenya, where I was located at the time.

I had a suspicion that this talk of war was completely rumor. I quickly found out that the "war" was in Uganda, so I hopped on a bus and headed in that direction. Sure enough, just across the border in Uganda, a newspaper headline read "War Rages in Western Uganda." Curiosity surpassed reason and I boarded a bus to western Uganda. The more westerly I traveled, the more the rumors diminished. Finally arriving in Mbarara, the supposed center of the war, I found the town peaceful. One shop owner had heard of a small skirmish among "a few boys with guns" up in the mountains behind the village. I had already realized that there was, in fact, no war, but I had come this far and I wanted to complete this mission, so I headed up into the hills on foot.

Before long, I saw three men in military fatigues carrying M-16 rifles. I tried to obscure myself behind a tree, but it was too late. One of the men noticed me, alerted the others, then walked directly toward me. Nowhere to run, I froze. The man stopped three feet from me and said "Go home," then turned and walked away. My desire to investigate this war quickly ended with that statement. I decided that that was a fitting end to my East Africa trip, so I took his advice, and a few days later I was home in L.A.

The point of the story is that we can't always trust what we hear or read in the media – even things that almost everyone agrees are true. Sometimes we need to search out alternative books, periodicals, voices, films, and even locations, in order to find the truth. Even though I found no war on that trip, it needs to be said that conflict to the degree of genocide is indeed occurring in Uganda. "Invisible Children" is an organization there that is pushing for change. Distortion or omission of information is just one of several ways that problems and their solutions are kept separate, and unnecessary suffering is allowed to perpetuate. In fact, through my travels and studies I had a gradual realization that truly surprised me: the technological solutions to the world's principal problems already exist. So then, the question comes, what on Earth is holding us back? And the answer is that nothing on Earth stands in our way. The tangible resolutions to our issues with energy, food, and disease are known and present – clear descriptions of which you will read in this book.

What is holding us back, therefore, is not external but internal. What restricts us is our fear-based beliefs about the world and how it works, and a simple lack of awareness about what's happening on the planet today. Mindsets have often proven to be more difficult to crash through than any physical barrier as the world has passed through its salient social transitions of racism, civil rights, sexism, and the yielding of dictatorship to democracy. In each case, fear had to be replaced with knowledge and awareness, exclusivity had to give way to understanding and inclusion, and those in power had to see that a more equitable system was better for all involved.

The same is true today and we as a planet must shift our mindset in order to see that uplifting the most downtrodden nations will help the entire world, and coming into harmony with the environment is necessary not just to maintain a high quality of life, but to continue any life at all. Broad societal beliefs which no longer serve us as a planet were defined in the introduction to this book. In this brief chapter, we will look more specifically at the attitudes and beliefs present within the two main participants or role players in this global social evolution: wealthy nations and poor nations. The focus of this chapter and in the first half of the book will be on the constrictive, or negative, beliefs in these regions, and how they produce conflict, lack, and hardship. The second half of the book will focus on the positive attitudes and beliefs that are generating material abundance, political harmony, and environmental healing.

The principal negative attitudes and emotions present in the developed, or wealthy, world are indulgence, avarice, myopia, and apathy. These are the source of countless actions that are harmful to the world. Fossil fuel burning and trash production are causing global warming, while our often unbridled consumption drives the sex and drug trades, animal poaching, and deforestation. Moreover, apathy among citizens of the West helps to perpetuate starvation, disease and unnecessary hardship in poor countries. Relatively small lifestyle changes and redirection of disposable income in the West could elevate the world's poorest to a respectable standard of living. In developing, or poorer nations, the palpable unhealthy attitudes and approaches of isolation, corruption, and desperation are also leading to harmful actions. Mismanagement of international aid money by third-world dictators cripples relief efforts, while deliberate political and cultural isolation hampers long-term economic and overall development. Also, desperate measures to survive, such as voluntary and involuntary participation in the sex trade and rampant deforestation, are propagating the spread of the AIDS virus and destroying tropical forests.

To be clear, the wealthy nations, also called the first world or the developed world, are comprised of the U.S., Canada, Japan, Australia, New Zealand, and most of the countries in Europe, especially western and northern Europe. Russia and China and a few oil economies of the Middle East are sometimes added to this group. Within this portion of the world, a very small group of politicians and corporate owners control the vast majority of resources and money. They employ much suppression of information, technology, and social awareness in order to exert control over tax revenues, financial markets, food production, and coveted resources such as oil. In several Western societies, tax money is used for war, which allows for military occupation and domination of nations with desirable resources, such as oil or drugs. Tax money is also shifted within the politico-economic oligarchy from government to big business in the form of subsidies and tax breaks. This small oligarchy, not exclusive to one political party, is very powerful and has much potential for good, but they are steeped in a fear-based mindset and hence are a very malevolent force on the planet.

The tangible solutions to the world's pressing problems are already here, and in some cases have been available for decades. But abundance for all means reduced profits and control for the few, so they will literally fight to the death to suppress solutions. Greed and myopia preclude the oligarchy's understanding of how their actions are damaging the environment and hurting the less fortunate. Even more, this greed keeps them focused on their own immediate needs, eschewing an acknowledgement of the long-term effects. Entering into a more harmonious world of less need, conflict and suffering means ending the world as the most powerful know and like it, so they resist bitterly.

In the words of author Alison Symington,

"Somehow, policy-makers and 'experts' have become adept at debating development as if it does not involve people, trade as if it is an end in itself, and international investment and production supply chains as if they are the only option. Most financial institutions and international economic actors talk of human rights as if they are unnecessary, purely political, confrontational, and really just a distraction from the important matters at hand. In fact, discussions often go on as if human rights do not exist, alternative models and values are absent and irrelevant, and by and large, humans and the environment are similarly irrelevant" (1).

A surreptitious but powerful expression of this is the existence of the International Monetary Fund (IMF), which is centered and controlled on the U.S. eastern seaboard. This institution and others like it, such as the World Bank, offer loans to the developing world yet with heavy contingencies. These so-called "structural adjustments" mandate that receiving nations open up their markets to vastly cheaper products from Western corporations, which makes domestic businesses and industries both unable to compete and vulnerable to foreign purchase. Thus, together with the World Trade Organization, the World Bank and IMF exude a unified commitment to what is called "neo-liberalism." Neo-liberalism is better named "old-conservatism" since it is based on "free" open markets, private ownership, export-focused development, and huge reductions in a government's spending on social services for its own people.

This approach is enriching transnational corporate CEOs and is making trade ledgers in wealthy nations favorable, yet it can be depleting and often devastating to fragile third-world economies. Also, it restricts these poor nations' evolution to the final stage of the "demographic transition" wherein economies can fully industrialize and fully develop, allowing their population growth rates to subside.

Under these economically repressive practices, these countries have skyrocketing populations coupled with beleaguered economies. This, not surprisingly, produces a palpable desperation, which is the dominant energy of the developing world. The startling pace at which the Earth's population is escalating is putting heavy pressure on resources such as food and clean water, and this is experienced most poignantly in the poorer countries.

This desperation amidst limited options for income in the developing world has led to literally hundreds of millions of people exercising one of the few options that they have left – to sell nature. Nature, in this case, takes many forms. As a part of the commodifiable natural environment, people's bodies themselves are put up for sale in the international labor and sex trades. Logging and the sale of lumber, or deforestation, is another commodification of nature in the absence of other avenues for income, while animal poaching for valuable hides and horns also abounds. Even beautiful vistas, beachfronts and coastlines are for sale and often abused through the tourism industry.

In 1996, I traveled by bus through a section of southern Brazil that was being deforested. I grew sick of the sweet, putrid smell of smoke from burning tropical forest that engulfed our bus for long stretches of the twenty-two hour drive. Unfortunately, that same smell greeted me in several other countries in the tropics.

This "nature for sale" degrades nature on many levels in the third world, and its consequences are experienced worldwide. Deforestation is a salient cause of global warming, and the sex trade is greatly exacerbating the spread of the HIV virus. Western companies further participate in this situation by deforesting large tracts of land for cash crop plantations and exploiting impoverished regions with the construction of slave-wage factories. Dire conditions in the developing world are also perpetuated by power-hungry leaders who embezzle national funds and isolate their countries culturally and economically. Zimbabwe, the Philippines, Myanmar, the Democratic Republic of Congo, and North Korea have been profoundly stunted by such rulers.

Another important player in this global scenario, beyond the major economic and governmental powers, is the general population in the developed, or wealthy, nations. Their awareness of the ills of global warming, government corruption, the food industry, and fossil fuels is growing, which is encouraging. Activism toward "going green," calling for government transparency, and supporting sustainable farming, for instance, is expanding significantly. However, a huge portion of first-world residents are still largely apathetic to these harmful trends. They have a vague awareness of the suffering, starvation, environmental crises, and war that most of the world is experiencing, but they feel no urgency to act and may implicitly hope that these problems will simply work themselves out. These individuals like to keep their attention on their small corner of the world, yet the issues that they ignore are increasingly affecting the foundation of all of our lives.

Those in this faction of American society are in danger of becoming the next idle American, or, if you will, the next American Idle. Rather than an American Idol singing star, they couple their sedentary lifestyle with their idle mindset and simply observe as their own health and the health of the planet deteriorates. It is my hope for those on the brink of becoming the next American Idle that they will become a true idol and leader by using the privilege of living in the world's most powerful country to take action – with their votes, their money, and their lifestyle choices - to change the world for the better on behalf of their fellow man.

The world is ever-changing and we must consistently take stock and assess our role in how our community and our world are functioning and evolving. Indeed, the beliefs, habits, and behaviors that are successful in one era are often not so amidst new circumstances. For instance, while America and many other nations were developing, the two specific ideals of individualism and self-reliance were prized and indeed necessary. Pioneers on the open frontier and political refugees in the thirteen colonies could not have survived without these philosophical pillars. They became central tenets of the Republican Party's platform, perhaps in part because of this obvious utility in the midst of a dynamic young nation. Yet we exist in a new America today. Manifest Destiny has been amply achieved, three-fourths of us live in urban areas, and the world is more connected and interdependent than at any time in history. Therefore, individualism and self-reliance, though still virtues, can actually hold us back in this new global reality.

These notions encourage us to think of the world as "us" vs. "them" and hence can encourage isolation, competition, and xenophobia. They can cut us off from the flow of commerce, ideas, and people that can improve and expand us. Individualism and self-reliance helped us to get where we are, but it is time to cultivate and emphasize a new view: a collective awareness that we are all connected and that our lives dramatically improve with the help and mutual cooperation of others. This belief is more current and advantageous for the existing planetary milieu. America must embrace its iconic ingenuity and dynamism – two of

its greatest exports – and allow them to inform the flexible
evolution of its ideologies and beliefs.

One core cause of many perennial societal ills, and a
topic which receives too little attention – is the control and
censorship of information. Directing the attention of wealthy
consumers in the first world is at the center of keeping the
capitalist economic machine running, and this frequently
entails both censorship and distraction. First, information
presented through the Western media is significantly filtered
by moneyed lobby groups, both conservative and liberal.
Many of these groups represent major industries such as auto
manufacturers, oil producers, and agribusiness. They put heavy
pressure on networks not to broadcast information that may
cast certain political or economic actions in a negative light.
This censorship can bring about provincialism by isolating the
population in first-world nations from certain global realities
and cultivating a dependence on the media to construct its
world view. Also contributing to this myopia is distraction
in the form of entertainment and fear. Over-stimulation and
entertainment – from 400 cable channels and sensationalized
"reality" TV shows to untold hours of internet surfing and
our daily coffee fix – together with the constant vague fear
of a terrorist attack distract the West very effectively from
cultivating a global awareness. Moreover, the U.S. and Europe
consume more recreational drugs, by far, than any other region
on Earth. This both produces an escape from reality and feeds
an insidious international drug trade.

A populace that consumes unabatedly is essential to
maintaining favorable traditional economic indicators, so
well-routinized efforts are aimed at keeping us unaware of
the negative environmental effects of our consumption in the
West. Remote landfills, obscuring the 500 billion pounds of
refuse that we in the U.S. produce annually, are one example.
Unmitigated consumption of gasoline, in particular, is fostered
through a proliferation of automobile ads and a conspicuous

lack of media coverage about the effects of burning fossil fuels on the environment and in producing global warming. The powerful thing about our copious consumption in the West is that it wields much influence over markets, industries, and resource supplies. Because of this, redirecting our consumption to companies that foster sustainability will, I believe, prove to be the source of our most effective environmental and social solutions.

In summation, in the West, unhealthy emotions of avarice and indulgence result in rampant fossil fuel burning, waste production, and denuding of natural environments. This co-mingles with population pressure and desperation which induces deforestation in the developing world. These dark emotions of avarice, disregard, and desperation, hence, are leading to the production of carbon dioxide, depletion of the ozone layer, and the removal of trees, our source of oxygen. Combined, these are generating a disease that is killing the earth: global warming.

Likewise, the pressure and desperation to survive in the developing world forces millions to disregard their own bodies and enter the sex trade. Meanwhile, ignorance, apathy, and a fostered disregard for "the other" allow the West to patronize the international sex and labor trades. Moreover, a broad umbrella of sexual repression in much of the world – the Puritanical foundation of the U.S. and female circumcision and general suppression of female sexuality in Africa and the Middle East – adds to this dark cocktail of attitudes about sexuality on a global scale. Thought, emotion, and intention comprise the seed and source of what we manifest as individuals and societies. Hence, it is not inconceivable that this sully mix of unhealthy emotions connected to sex has contributed to the coalescence and global spread of AIDS. The proliferation of our unhealthy emotions toward our bodies, together with disregard and abuse of nature, are abetting a disease of the body – AIDS – and a disease of the Earth –

global warming.

Without an analysis of the source of these global-scale ailments, solving them has proven difficult and delayed. These "diseases" are not accidents, nor have they come from nowhere. They are the long-developed accumulation and materialization of attitudes and circumstances that in some part, we ourselves have chosen and propagated. When our fear of a lack of power, money, and resources subsides, and when we achieve an increased awareness of our planet and of the injustices that we commit against it and against each other, this shroud over our planet of mistreatment and hardship can fall away. In this way, the light of day can shine through and these problems can begin to be solved and healed.

Human Traffic

"Those who deny freedom to others deserve it not for themselves…This is a world of compensations; and he who would be no slave, must consent to have no slave."

-Abraham Lincoln, April 6, 1859, Letter to Henry Pierce

The following is a real-life profile taken from Campagna and Poffenberger's *The Sexual Trafficking in Children: an investigation of the child sex trade:*

"On August 1, 1984, an older white male was arrested by police officers of New York City's 7th Precinct for sexually abusing a nine-year-old Mexican boy. The child, Luis, had been registered two or three days earlier at a summer day camp on New York's lower east side by the same man.

An observant youth worker noticed that Luis was depressed, crying, and walking as though in pain. She took him aside and asked what was wrong. The story, as told to investigators from Defense for Children International – USA, was that Luis was born in Acapulco, Mexico. The father of his large and very poor family was approached three weeks before by a visiting Anglo who offered to take the boy to New York, provide him with an education, teach him English, and eventually find him a job. An unknown amount of money changed hands and Luis was brought to the United States, without proper documentation, past immigration officials. The effect on Luis of such a change in environment, from sunny Acapulco to the lower east side of New York, was doubtless traumatic. He had been separated from family, friends, school, his entire way of life, only to become a victim of sexual assault" (1).

Trafficking in people for prostitution is one of the fastest-growing areas of international criminal activity and one of the sites of increasing concern to the United States and to the international community. Sex trafficking is the voluntary and involuntary transportation of people across international borders in order to enter the sex trade. According to FBI, UN, and UNESCO general estimates, between 700,000 and two million people are trafficked each year worldwide (2)(3). Of those, approximately 70% are female and 50% are children (4).

Trafficking is the third largest source of profits for organized crime – third only to arms and drugs – and it generates $25 to $32 billion each year (5)(6). The majority of this activity has gone on throughout Asia for the past few decades, but now there is a shift, due to increased government regulations and protection of sex workers, namely in Sri Lanka and Thailand. These activities have largely been diverted to elsewhere on the globe where cultures and economic situations are well-positioned to receive such an industry. Latin America and Africa are the main sites that are receiving this new flow of sex business, and hence, demand for sex workers.

If women and children who enter the sex trade to satisfy demand only within their own country are included in this equation, the total numbers involved are much higher globally. The prominence of children who are forced into the sex trade in India was highlighted in "Slumdog Millionaire," which won the 2009 Oscar for best film of the year.

This international sex trade is caused and perpetuated, in large part, by three specific and pervasive global attitudes. The first is the judgment and suppression of sexuality. Repression of sex on several levels and in many of the world's cultures limits and stifles sexuality, coaxing it to erupt in perversions and tweaked expressions such as sexual violence, pedophilia, the multi-billion-dollar cyber-sex industry, and the sex trade. This repression itself, ironically, generates the draw and profitability of the sex trade. When sexuality is not allowed avenues of acceptable expression, there is a creation of a false sense of scarcity of sex. Men, especially, often come to believe that they must search for sex, pay for it, or even use violence to get it – and yet it is something that is so abundant and intrinsically human. This is very similar to the belief in the idea of scarcity of energy and food, while unlimited renewable energy awaits our use and food surpluses spoil all over the world.

The second attitudinal trend which could be said to contribute to the existence of the sex trade is the greed among the wealthiest in the first world for ever more resources and power. Coupled with the fear of losing what they already have, this greed generates the need to dominate and suppress others. This is expressed in the economic subjugation of the developing world by first-world powers. The resultant crippled third-world economies leave residents desperate to survive. One result of this desperation is the tidal wave of both willing and unwilling participation in the sex trade. Several nations which are not subjected to this domination, such as parts of economically-depressed Eastern Europe, are also providing sex trade workers in large numbers.

The third energetic trend that helps to generate this trade is excessive masculine or "yang" energy, which leads to male chauvinism and domination. The result is the global denigration of women and their status as second-class citizens in the majority of the world's nations. The United Nations publishes a Gender Related Development Index (GDI) and a Gender Empowerment Measure (GEM) which are used in its annual Human Development Report to determine a country's level of gender equality. A score of 1.0 is perfect gender equality. Norway (0.94) topped the list, while Niger (0.26) was at the bottom. Many countries in Africa are in the 0.5 range, while innumerable nations are between 0.6 and 0.75 globally (7). What this translates to is that women on this planet have less access to education, money, free expression, social status, and perhaps most of all, power. The sex trade, when spurred by poverty in the area, is a natural extension of this role of women as subjugated, used, and lacking power. Women's subjugation by men is paralleled by the developing world's subjugation by the West, whereas the subjugated offers their body (sex and labor) or natural fecundity (minerals and resources) to the dominant power.

Amidst the utter denigration of selling their bodies, women are also ironically elevated in importance and efficacy because of their new role as providers for the family. In beleaguered developing-world economies, this expanded income, mostly sourced from first-world patrons, posits women on an entirely new level in society. Despite the source of this money, sex workers often have pride in their observably moneyed status. They become the supporter of their families, including brothers and husbands. Considering that in several destitute countries there are over a million female sex workers with a stream of income, this constitutes a gigantic shift in gender roles, and in the power of women in general. Additional discussion about the lives of women around the world is found within this book in the chapter entitled "The Rise of Women."

While researching the sex industry in Thailand, I interviewed prostitutes, their "managers," and U.S. military personnel on leave in Thai port cities. When asked what their job was, several women were reticent to speak, but a few of these girls and women seemed to sit up straighter when they said "I am a prostitute," almost with a glint of pride. When they learned that I was an American scholar researching the Thai economy and sex trade, two of the women even invited me to meet their parents and families. This is a small bit of evidence of how beautiful, flexible, and accepting the Thai culture is, even amidst the vicissitudes of an unsavory industry.

Many women do voluntarily enter the sex trade, but a huge proportion of them do so by coercion by a variety of methods including outright kidnapping and exportation, lure by phony job offers in foreign countries, or false marriage opportunities with Westerners that are advertised in local papers. All of these mechanisms are used to dupe women into accepting transport to another country, where the story changes and the institution of debt bondage is enacted. The transported women are told that they owe in upwards of 30,000 U.S. dollars for the cost of their transport, which they can pay off by working in sex bars or brothels. These women are essentially enslaved: monitored twenty-four hours a day and forced to acquiesce to all clients' demands. Debts are usually paid in a few to several months (8). Some organizations estimate that workers can earn their captors between $13,000 and $67,000 per year (9).

This debt dependence is used as a tool of the dominant group, or "hegemon," throughout history and across cultures. After slavery ended in the United States, blacks in the south commonly entered into the sharecropping system in which they rented land at rates too high to be paid back with the crops that they grew, so they were perpetually in debt and subjected to the demands of the land owner. The IMF and World Bank use a very similar strategy with large loans to the developing world which allow the lending institutions to control and manipulate these economies at their will while debt dependence is still in effect. Another parallel is that in the African slave trade and the modern sex trade, the wrangling and selling of local victims to Western powers is often facilitated by locals of the same tribe or ethnic group as the victim.

Governments play a crucial role in the perpetuation of this industry as well. There is a chosen myopia and active ignorance of the problem, as if governments just hope it goes away. First, there are inadequate international laws, in that penalties for trafficking in humans are often minor compared to trafficking in arms or drugs.

The lack of official acknowledgement of the sex trade itself precludes the granting of official "worker" visas to sex workers. Hence they are subject to all manner of human rights violations and are not protected by local law enforcement, nor eligible for public health care.

Also, on a national scale, punishment of sex workers is much more common than punishment of traffickers. In the case of Thai migrant workers in Japan, "if employers or traffickers are prosecuted at all, they are charged with immigration offenses, the employment of illegal aliens, or with operating an unlicensed entertainment business. They are almost never prosecuted for the severe human rights abuses they have committed, such as forced labor, illegal confinement, and physical violence" (10). Moreover, anti-prostitution or anti-illegal immigration laws directed at the victims only exacerbate the problem by increasing the profitability of the industry. In countries where prostitution is legal, trafficking is less common and the sex industry is more regulated (11).

The Asia Migrant Bulletin has documented the trafficking of migrants from the Philippines, Thailand, China, Indonesia, Burma, Sri Lanka, Bangladesh, India, Nepal, and of late from Vietnam, Laos, Cambodia, and Fiji. These sex workers were sent to the nations of Japan, Taiwan, Hong Kong, Macao, Malaysia, Singapore, Thailand, India, Australia, Europe, and the United States (12). Yet as stated earlier, there has been a diminishment of sex trade activity in Thailand and Sri Lanka, two main centers of the trade, due to greater awareness and stronger laws in those countries. Sex commerce has shifted principally to Latin America, the Caribbean, and Africa. These newly engaged regions are susceptible and "primed" for this invasion of money and domination because of their depressed economies and also due to the strong tradition of male dominance and patrilinealism in these regions.

Approximately 50,000 women from the Dominican Republic currently work abroad in the European sex industry, mainly in Austria, Germany, Greece, Italy, and the Netherlands (13). The following is a quotation about poverty as a cause of sex trade activity in the Dominican Republic. "In the case of Dominican women, the proceeds from prostitution are used to support parents or children. For those women really concerned about providing such support, opportunities in the legal economy are very limited in a society where eighty dollars a month is the minimum salary for domestic work" (14).

With an undergirding of so much repression and denouncement of sexuality imposed upon the women of the world, feelings of guilt, self-denial, sacrifice, and shame are a logical experience for women selling their bodies for sex. Also, from the other side of this equation, guilt, disregard, and domination are the energetic foundation of the (mostly, though not all, Western) men wanting to set loose their sexual desires on helpless or even coerced victims. None of the feelings and attitudes that these role players in the sex trade bring to an encounter could be described as positive, pleasant, or "healthy." It is widely accepted in the developed world that emotional and mental stress are the leading cause of illness. That is, one's mental and emotional state, more often than other factors, creates physical illnesses. Therefore it is certainly possible, and in fact plausible, that these unhealthy emotions and mental attitudes that are infused into the sex trade may actually contribute to the physical manifestation of diseases such as AIDS. David R. Hawkins, M.D., Ph.D, is a world renowned psychiatrist and has also co-authored a book with Linus Pauling. On the metaphysics of AIDS, Dr. Hawkins writes:

"Generally it appears that what's experienced as stress results in suppression of the thymus gland, and the body's defenses are consequently impaired. But the various research approaches to this topic fail to examine the relationship between belief systems and attitudes, and the resulting context of perception that determines the nature of individual experience" (15).

Regions where suppression, domination, and guilt related to sex are most prominent often display higher rates of disease. Legal and social openness about sex and the sex trade, for instance, results in psychological changes (empowerment and autonomy for women) and tangible changes (doctor visits and condom distribution), which can combine to lower transmission rates (16).

One extreme example is in southern Africa, which has the highest concentration of people with AIDS on Earth. In a few countries in this region, 20% or more of the adult population has the disease (17). I saw this first-hand when, on a bus passing through Uganda in the late 90s, I glimpsed a giant admonishing sign posted on the roadside as we approached a town which read simply "One-third of this town has HIV." Of note, women's rates of AIDS in the region often approach double that of men's. If we look at the extreme "dis-ease" with sex that women in the region have imposed upon them, the prominence of the sex-related disease of AIDS is perhaps more understandable.

In the words of Pulitzer-Prize winning science author Laurie Garrett, who has been covering the AIDS epidemic since the mid-1990s, "The number one driving force for this epidemic in Sub Saharan Africa and increasingly in Asia is the extraordinarily low power balance on the side of females. Most women have no right of refusal of sexual intercourse. They have no ability to dictate when, where or with whom they have sex. Rape is so commonplace that it is only recently being thought of as a criminal activity" (18).

This energy of sexual suppression and mistreatment among African women is so extreme and visceral in Africa that it frequently results in the death of women. A woman who commits adultery is often severely beaten or burned and fiercely judged or ostracized. In situations of infidelity, the murder of a woman by her husband is often not strictly forbidden or monitored. Rape is so common that many marriages begin when a woman is raped by an acquaintance. Rape is also a tool of demoralization and power which is commonly utilized in civil wars on the continent. One cultural phenomenon in sub-Saharan Africa – female genital mutilation, or female circumcision – is a vivid and extreme example of the sexual mistreatment of women. Often at the age of eight to ten, young girls in Africa have their clitoris scraped off with blunt traditional, non-medical instruments. The procedure is called "purification" because of its effect of diminishing the woman's ability to experience sexual pleasure, thereby lowering her libido and better ensuring fidelity to her husband. UNICEF estimates that 70 million girls aged 15-49 in Africa and the Middle East have undergone the procedure (19). Although sixteen African nations now ban the practice (20), approximately three million new girls still face the prospect of female circumcision each year (21). This level of sexual suppression and physical abuse aligns with the general precepts of the sex trade, making African women very susceptible to the industry.

On the macro-commercial level, the human sex trafficking industry generates up to $32 billion a year for organized crime (22). A notable Thai economist has estimated that the annual income generated by Thai sex workers in Japan alone is 310,500 million yen, or U.S. $3.3 billion (23). Traffickers are from all over the world: gangs from China, Mexico, Central America, and Russia as well as Chinese and

Vietnamese triads, the Japanese Yakuza, South American drug cartels, and the Italian Mafia (24).

As in the cases of drugs and arms, the United States is getting involved in this huge illicit flow of cash and product. On the surface, of course, the intent is purported to be benevolent, yet with a glance at the policies of the last few presidential administrations' approaches to the issue, some clear variances from benevolence are detectible:

1. First, in the Bush plan, in 2002 the U.S. Attorney General announced the implementation of special "T" visas for undocumented victims of trafficking in the United States who cooperate with U.S. law enforcement officials by divulging identities of their traffickers. They are granted permission to stay in the United States.

2. Second, in the same year, Bush signed an executive order creating an inter-agency task force to "monitor and combat trafficking in persons." This task force is heavily stocked with political and intelligence power, and it includes: the Secretary of State, the Attorney General, the Secretary of Labor, the Director of the CIA, and the Office of the National Security Advisor.

3. Third, the Department of Justice was commissioned to institute training programs for federal prosecutors, INS personnel, and FBI agents aimed at locating human traffickers.

4. In early 2003, Attorney General John Ashcroft indicated that since passage of the U.S. anti-trafficking legislation the year before, the U.S. Department of Justice has doubled the number of

prosecutions and convictions for trafficking (25).

So, looking at the Bush plan, it seems substantial, focused, and a serious call to arms against this cause. Yet when we look at the Clinton plan from a few years earlier, the Bush administration's focus on punishment and an apparent interest in finding the flow of cash in this industry becomes manifest. Clinton's plan has a completely different emphasis.

The Clinton plan and related goals were as follows:

1. Increase economic opportunities for potential victims, increase public awareness of trafficking dangers and the entity of human trafficking in general.

2. Generate legislation to provide shelter and support services to victims who are in this country unlawfully and therefore ineligible for public assistance. (No need to disclose trafficking bosses in order to receive assistance from the Clinton administration).

3. Press for legislation that enacts the possibility of restitution for trafficked victims through bringing private civil lawsuits against traffickers. Discover legislative ways to go after and prosecute traffickers and increase penalties that they can face (26).

The difference in the impetus and philosophy behind these two plans is substantial. There is certainly something to be said for the hard-nosed, punitive Bush plan approach. Yet the compassion and emphasis on solving the problem at its source in Clinton's plan is notable. Perhaps a combination of the two plans would be optimal. To its credit, the Bush administration provided $100 million to over 100 countries to aid in the amelioration of the trafficking in women (27). However, the U.S. government's hundreds of millions of dollars put into the Latin American and Asian drug trades and the copious evidence of our spurious and clandestine involvement in both locations casts our new-found interest in sex trafficking in a questionable light. Military involvement or financial investment, other than aid, by our government in another country in the last several decades can certainly elicit reserved circumspection.

Statistics, legislation, and governmental policies related to the sex trade help to elucidate the larger problem, but a true story of a victim of the forces at play in the global sex industry can have a different, more human impact. Coercion takes on many forms, from being directly abducted to essentially finding oneself at the mercy of circumstance: destitute, with a lack of education and opportunity, and confronted with the sole promising yet uninspiring option of selling one's own body. Throughout my travels and research, I have encountered many girls and women in this exact situation in the developing world, but a brief conversation with two girls in Nairobi, Kenya in the late 90s left me speechless and with no educated retort.

"They can't be older than fifteen," I remember saying to myself when I saw two school girls strolling a boulevard in the outskirts of the two million-plus metropolis in southern Kenya. Their aggressive, over-confident stares propositioning male passers-by divulged their profession. Having just finished my first year of teaching at an inner-city high school in Los Angeles, these two girls looked like sophomores in my class that should be talking about homework or the prom. My heart went out to them, and I had to reach out. I walked up to them and, just to be sure, respectfully asked if they were prostitutes. Without a hint of shame, they both nodded.

"I have a question to ask but I'm not sure how to ask it," I said. Their eyebrows raised, waiting. I continued.

"Wouldn't you rather just work at the post office or at a bank or a restaurant, rather than have to risk so much out here?"

The more courageous of the two immediately took a step toward me and pointed her index finger at me.

"I will tell you why we don't have jobs like that." Her boldness took me aback. As she continued, her East African accent was more detectable. "My motha is a teacha and she makes feefty dollars a month. I have already made feefty dollars tooday, and on a good day I will make 200 dollars." I found myself with nothing to say. It's tough to argue with a disparity like that, so I just nodded and said "Well… be safe out here," and I left. My heart sank more with every step as I fully comprehended the inevitability of their situation. It is the prerogative of citizens in nations that have the power to make change not only to police traffickers who force women and children into the sex trade, but also to earnestly work to change the seminal social and economic circumstances that can be just as oppressive and just as frightening.

Our Exploding Population

In 1930 the Earth's population had finally reached two billion people. By 1960 that number doubled, and by 1995 it doubled again. It had required the entirety of human history for the population to reach two billion people and then in approximately one human lifetime, it went from two billion to six billion people (1). Most mid-range estimates predict that our population will peak at anywhere from nine to eleven billion inhabitants within the next century.

Several specific social and technological changes are at the source of this population explosion which is changing conditions and realities on the Earth at breakneck speed. Even though by casual observation it may be difficult to see or palpably feel this change on a daily basis, the tidal wave of growth is quickly modifying the natural world, as well as the way that we will live our lives from now on. Life on this little spaceship called Earth is changing fast, and many more of us need to get out of the passenger seat and into the driver's seat if we are to turn the ship around in time.

The main concern related to the rising number of human beings is that all of these new people will require water, food, and energy, while many of these resources are finite. Fresh water supplies are actually decreasing due to glacial melting and overdrawing of groundwater, fossil fuels are rapidly running out, and the amount of arable (farmable) land on the planet shrinks every year due to desertification, over-farming, and expansion of cattle grazing. Wars are being fought at this very moment over oil, but even more fervor will charge the conflicts of the future over water, with thirty-one countries already facing critical fresh water shortages.

For most of human history – some 200,000 years -- the population of the planet hovered steadily at around 200 million people. In the late 18th and 19th centuries medical knowledge improved and death rates began to plummet, which allowed the population to skyrocket. During the next century, several nations industrialized, their people moved from farms to cities, and with urbanism, birthrates fell. This dramatically slowed or halted population growth in these countries. Yet most of the world has not made this final transition to industrialized urban life, so populations continue to escalate rapidly since a rural, agricultural lifestyle carries huge incentives for having multiple children.

The key to understanding and solving this rampant population growth lies in the concept of the "demographic transition." In this transition, each society goes through four stages of evolution. In a Stage One society, birthrates are high because the society is based on agriculture or hunting and gathering, so it is advantageous to have many children who can serve as laborers. Death rates, however, are also high because medical knowledge and access to medical care is limited and food supplies are often inconsistent. The high birth and death rates balance each other out and the population does not grow significantly. This describes Europe in the Middle Ages, countless ancient civilizations, and only a handful of modern tribal or nomadic societies.

Many nations entered Stage Two of the demographic transition in the 19th century when advancements in medicine, such as the understanding of bacteria and the circulatory system, and eventually the invention of antibiotics and vaccines, dramatically increased life expectancies over much of the planet. Availability of new seeds and foods, such as potatoes and tomatoes from the Americas, brought diversification of crops and helped to decrease the frequency of famine. These factors lowered death rates significantly, yet birth rates were still high since most nations were still heavily engaged in agriculture. Therefore, populations soared.

The Industrial revolution itself comprises Stage Three of the demographic transition. Four factors must exist in order for an industrial revolution to occur: capital accumulation (money), a substantial faction of idle laborers, a surplus of food, and manufacturing technology (steel smelting, steam engines, etc.). The development of industry and the pursuant creation of factories fundamentally alters a society by drawing workers from farms to work in factories located in dense urban areas. This critical shift immediately slows birth rates because there are countless forces in city life that discourage the bearing of children, such as expensive urban amenities like rent, food, school, transportation, and entertainment. Family planning education and materials are available, and moreover, the obligations of child rearing compete with the expanding possibility of a career. All of which lower birth rates.

In Stage Four, a society fully industrializes and urbanizes, and its population growth slows, shrinks, or simply halts. The penultimate example has been occurring in Eastern Europe for decades. Currently nearly every country in Europe, along with Japan, the USA, Canada, New Zealand, Australia, and a few other nations have completed the demographic transition and now are in Stage Four with very low or negative growth rates (when immigration statistics are not figured in). The nations of Mexico, Thailand, and China are examples of populations that are transitioning from Stage Three to Stage Four, but have not yet fully arrived and slowed their growth sufficiently.

However, most of the world is still "stuck" in Stage Two of this evolution and their populations continue to vault at upwards of 2% per year, meaning they double in size about every 35 years. This includes most of Latin America and Africa, much of the Middle East, and southern Asia. Many of these countries are urbanizing rapidly, which would seem to indicate development. Yet because of how it is occurring, it actually is evidence of the opposite. People are moving from rural to urban areas in the developing world in such large numbers, in fact, that it constitutes the largest migration in human history. Yet these migrants are not being pulled to cities by industrialization and jobs; rather, they are being pushed from countrysides which are no longer able to support such massive and growing populations. The result is the emerging presence of giant slums or squatter settlements outside of so-called megacities throughout the developing world. These cities are little more capable of dealing with these destitute masses than are the rural areas. Hence, rural emigrants simply cluster into makeshift settlements on the outskirts of urban areas with informal housing, no sewage or electricity, and normally without paved roads. Cities such as Mumbai, Sao Paolo, and Mexico City hover near twenty million inhabitants. Delhi, Rio de Janeiro, Dhaka, Manila, Seoul, Karachi, Cairo, and Kolkata (Calcutta) are close behind and growing fast (2).

These slums are riddled with violence, drugs, and deplorable sanitation conditions, as evidenced in the films *Slumdog Millionaire* (set in Mumbai) and *City of God* (set in Rio de Janeiro). I personally encountered the favelas, or slums, of Sao Paolo and Rio de Janeiro in 1996 as I was traveling from Iguacu Falls (Foz do Iguacu) in southern Brazil to the east and up the coast of the country. Approaching both of these Brazilian megalopolises from their hinterland, our bus first encountered mile after mile of shanty-towns with shelters made of cardboard, plastic sheeting, corrugated metal, and the occasional cinder block structure. These vast agglomerations stretched seemingly interminably with the city proper only a distant sight. A visitor entering and exiting the city through the main airport does not ever have to pass through and experience these parts of megacities where the least fortunate on our planet reside.

Due in large part to their rapidly expanding slums, several cities in Africa are growing at close to 4% per year, meaning their populations will double in less than twenty years. Dar es Salaam, Tanzania; Nairobi, Kenya; Luanda, Angola; and Kinshasa of the Democratic Republic of Congo are examples.

These particular ramifications of population growth are not a surprise to some. In 1798, English Parson and economist Thomas Malthus made a famous proclamation that since people multiply exponentially (1,2,4,8,16, etc.) while agricultural production multiplies arithmetically, (1,2,3,4,5, etc.) the Earth would soon encounter an acute scarcity of food. As testament to this prediction, currently on the Earth, some 15,000 people die of starvation every day, while 48 countries comprising 2.8 billion people are expected to face fresh water shortages by 2025 (3). Moreover, 40% of the world lives on less than the equivalent of US $2 per day (4). Hence this prognosticated "Malthusian Crisis" over limited resources has certainly arrived. However, it has been mitigated and delayed significantly by advancements in farm technology such as the green revolution of the 1980's, which employed genetically engineered seeds and heavy chemical inputs in order to increase yields -- sometimes up to three-fold. Bill Gates continues to fund such projects which have the mixed result of producing more life-saving food, yet indenturing farmers to pesticide and fertilizer-company loans. Food output has increased so significantly that throughout the past century, famine is more commonly a result of political power-plays and a lack of distribution of food than of insufficient production (5). This is all the more troubling when we consider how many people unnecessarily starve to death daily. Yet, the massive chemical inputs necessary to increase yields have unfortunately left millions of acres of soil heavily polluted or depleted from over-farming, which threatens future harvests.

A harmony must be attained between the sustainability of organic farming techniques and the high output of the Gates-funded green revolution technologies. Our impressive solutions to feeding the escalating global populace have changed what we thought possible, yet these approaches still are not viable as long-term solutions if they are not made more sustainable. Using fewer chemical additives and infusing fields with local composted food and plant waste, as opposed to expensive chemical-laden petroleum-based fertilizers, are ways to conserve and fortify our precious life-giving soils. Besides in hydroponic and similar environments, food needs soil in order to grow, and soil is a non-renewable resource, at least on the human timescale.

A very general estimate shows that, disregarding sedimentation, in a given region the Earth produces about one inch of good soil every 500 years. In conjunction, most crops require at least six inches of soil to take root. Therefore, if a society ruins the upper two to three inches of "topsoil" over millions of square miles each year annually through conventional chemical farming, then the soils over massive regions will require 1,000 to 1,500 years to fully naturally reproduce and restructure themselves. That timeline is mortally slow if you live in an area where soils are currently too depleted to grow food. Our soils need to be cared for like the precious gift that they are – the source of our livelihood here on Earth.

When discussing our survivability on planet Earth, one simple habit is causing more than its fair share of problems -- eating beef. Already 20% of the land surface of the Earth is accessible to grazing cattle, and over one-third of deforestation in the Amazon forest is to make space for cattle ranches or to grow soy to be fed to cattle (6). Also, nearly half of all grain grown on Earth is fed to cattle, not humans. Therefore, as global beef consumption escalates, less and less of the world's grain harvest is available to our starving populations (7). Moreover, the beef industry worldwide produces about 65% and 37% of anthropogenic nitrous oxide and methane, respectively, which are both several-fold more causative of global warming than CO2 (8). There is more discussion of beef later in the "Living More Efficiently" chapter.

Though great strides in our husbandry of resources are necessary, even perfect husbandry of our soils and resources will not fully assuage our food and resource supply problems. The crux of this issue lies in the regions of the world which are still stuck in Stage Two of the demographic transition, comprising two-thirds of the planet, where populations are soaring. These countries and the reasons why their economies have not fully industrialized are worthy of much investigation. Realizing that, in essence, an industrial revolution is an economic phenomenon, it becomes clear that helping these nations to evolve and advance economically is the key to industrialization, and hence, to their population urbanizing and their growth rates slowing.

Yet it is precisely the economic rise of the third-world that first-world capitalists and industrialists quite actively eschew, because simply, this invites competition. It makes no sense in traditional capitalism to help another company or nation to advance. Therefore, within that framework, transnational corporations cannot be fully faulted for trying to garner and maintain dominance over developing economies. Yet environmentally, socially, morally, and collectively, it makes perfect sense – urgent sense – to indeed aid these economies and nations to progress. The espousal of an expanded view and a new definition of "progress" is needed for the globe to identify this critical point in the evolution of our symbiosis with the Earth. The notion of progress must be expanded beyond economic indicators to take in our social, cultural, and biological *survival* on the planet. Moreover, corporate espousal of collaboration, philanthropy, and environmentalism is rapidly emerging as a dependable avenue to larger profits.

Pure capitalists may be partially forgivable but they nonetheless, along with nations, leaders, and supranational organizations such as the World Bank, IMF, and World Trade Organization (WTO), are in positions of responsibility. They have an obligation, if you will, to do the right thing, to steer us in a wise collectively minded direction, and to call for small sacrifices in order to deliver grand and broad-based abundance. The IMF and World Bank have been ambivalent about this calling, at times proving to be wise and selfless and at others myopic and self-serving.

In recent decades, much lending to the developing world from these two institutions has come laden with heavy conditions, mentioned in an earlier chapter. These include de-nationalizing businesses so they are available for sale to foreign buyers, and removing import taxes on foreign goods so that local goods no longer have a competitive advantage. These measures sometimes prove to be precisely the kind of direct influence that is stalling struggling economies and trapping these nations in Stage Two of the demographic transition: not yet fully industrialized and urbanized, and hence with skyrocketing populaces.

Affecting change at this scale can prove out of reach for the average citizen, though related protests at recent G8 (Group of Eight) and G20 (Group of Twenty) conferences in Edinburgh and Genoa, for instance, have had a noted impact. Supporting leaders of these wealthy nations who display fairness, open-mindedness, and the courage to look at issues at the global and long-term scales is our prerogative. We can elect officials in the U.S. and in other wealthy nations who see that uplifting other countries and economies displays vastly more power than debilitating them. We are at a place where this approach is quickly becoming the only way to allow life, progress, and a future for most of the world's people. Anything less than widespread cooperation and concerted focus on coming together to solve our global problems will only continue the slide toward our eventual demise. It is too easy to decide from a table in Starbucks or a corner office with a view to "prudently" advance American interests in the developing world and allow the prosperity to "trickle down" to those in these beleaguered developing world regions. Only from a location so distanced from the true suffering could economists and politicians make such unrealistic and cold calculations.

It is my belief that those in power will increasingly realize that we are all one large interconnected society, one giant fused ecosystem, one interdependent economy and family who rely on each other and intimately affect every single other on the planet. Seeing ourselves as independent, competitive entities and societies is leaving hundreds of millions starving and it constitutes turning our back on the environment and allowing it to deconstruct.

Perhaps we will start to see that we are on this tiny craft flying through space and, whether we like it or not, we are all working together. Again employing the analogy of an airplane, we need all of our parts to function in order for us to fly. All peoples of the globe need to sustainably live with their local environment and need to offer their unique knowledge, ingenuity and skills in order for this global milieu to function optimally. Currently, a few wealthy entities sit in the cockpit and attempt to keep most of the food, resources, and power to themselves. But they must give fuel to the engines (global industry) and deliver power to operate the wing and tail steering (the United Nations, WTO, etc.), as well as honor the knowledge of passengers as navigators and co-pilots (democratic representation). Without this, we shall never get off the ground and realize that we are infinitely more than we now perceive ourselves to be, and that we cannot experience our true greatness and destiny until we support, acknowledge, and include all aspects of our wholeness.

When we begin to fly, the small, self-focused gains that we used to clamor for will seem laughable when compared to our expanded new reality. The rising population of the globe is a critical and pressing problem. Economic avarice is proving a significant hurdle to pushing a large portion of the world to the next stage of the demographic transition so that their birth rates may subside. Hopefully, the reality of our inter-connectedness will continue to manifest itself and we will individually, nationally, and collectively take action to slow population growth and claim our grander future.

The So-Called "Drug War"

"One does not establish a dictatorship in order to safe-guard a revolution; one makes a revolution in order to establish a dictatorship."

- George Orwell

"Cuando llegaste a este pais? (When did you arrive in this country?)

"Y tu pasaporte, por que no esta estampado? (And why isn't your passport stamped?)

Less than 100 miles from the Colombian border, my mind was reeling as I sat in an Ecuadorian military center being interrogated as a suspected drug smuggler. Seated in the middle of a dark room with a light pointed at my face, I was being drilled with questions in Spanish by an apparently high-ranking Ecuadorian military officer (based on his impressively decorated uniform).

"Hace cuanto tiempo que estas en Ecuador? (How long have you been in Ecuador?)

I did my best to answer the questions but an accidental double-vaccination for yellow fever a month prior had basically induced the symptoms of yellow fever and it was blurring my memory along with other mental faculties. This only exacerbated the fact that my story, though truthful, sounded very fabricated. I had walked from northern Peru into Ecuador, so I never passed through an official customs station.

I was trying to sound credible as the officer paced in circles around me, but it was clear that he thought I had purchased drugs in Colombia, crossed the border illegally, and was trying to utilize Quito airport's less stringent security as a way of getting off of the continent.

So there I sat, pleading my case for freedom in my second language, with no way to contact another soul who could help me, fighting the symptoms of yellow fever, and not knowing what would possibly happen next.

I suppose that something in my eyes or the tone of my voice or body language finally gave him confidence in my story because my interrogator suddenly stopped pacing and said that they would stamp my passport and allow me to leave the country. But first, I would pay a "very big fine." I wildly imagined what the fine could be for suspected drug smuggling. In the end I had to hold back a smile as I was paying my fine of 1,000 Ecuadorian Sucres, which amounted to about U.S. $3.30.

I had gotten lucky, but I didn't realize at the time how extensive, pervasive, and multi-lateral the drug wars are in South America, Mexico, and Afghanistan. Nor did I understand how intimately involved the United States is on all levels of the industry.

The South American drug war has received much attention in the past three decades because it involves the flow of billions of dollars, principally between the U.S. and Colombia. Increasingly of late, the transport of these drugs into the U.S. has led to a dramatic increase in drug cartel violence throughout Mexico and along the U.S./Mexico border. Moreover, Afghanistan's position as the world's largest producer of heroin has drawn hundreds of millions of dollars of attention from the United States government and military as an important aspect of the war there. Overall, the UN estimates that selling drugs in the United States, the world's largest drug consumer, amounts to $142 billion in annual business (1).

Yet the prototype for U.S. involvement with a drug production zone exists in the past three decades in Colombia, Peru, and Bolivia. The strategies that we have employed there are being played out now in both Mexico and Afghanistan. The United States government has entered this South American arena to a significant degree through substantial financial and military involvement. Particularly since the beginning of U.S. intervention, it is increasingly difficult to determine what's going on below the surface of rhetoric, distracting and disorienting activities, and shifting alliances in this hotbed of money and multi-directional conflict.

The stated goals of the United States in the drug war in South America have been to cultivate democracy, support human rights, and curb the production of cocaine and other drugs at the source. Its principal method of achieving these goals, observably, has been the militarization of Latin America through what are called U.S. Security Assistance Programs. These programs include four basic elements: direct monetary funding for national militaries, supply of military technology and equipment, training by the U.S. armed forces, and strategic advice from the United States government.

Immediately there seems to be a contradiction between the humanitarian, benevolent publicly-stated goals of the government, and the aggressive, militarily-focused approach that is actually being employed. In a war of such inherent deception and clandestine motives, it is often more fruitful to look at the tangible results of such an intervention rather than trying to sift through rhetoric for some solid truth.

Taking this approach, there are four main results that are consistently seen as a result of the U.S. Security Assistance Programs. First, countries in the region are destabilized because the expanded national militaries check and surpass the power of national governments. There are frequent assassinations of anti-drug politicians, and martial (military) law is often imposed in times of "emergency." This chronology in the country of Colombia, the center of the drug trade, shows a strong correlation between U.S. involvement, militarization, and the promotion of the drug trade.

In 1982, President Belisario Betancur is elected, and in 1983 he rejects the U.S. supported extradition treaty (to oust drug czars from the country). In following, the U.S. imposes heavy economic sanctions on Colombia – mainly flowers, perishable goods, and the airlines were affected (2). In 1984, in response to guerilla activity, the Colombian legislature deems the country to be in a state of siege, which greatly expands military and police power (reminiscent of the post 9/11 Patriot Act) (3). During this U.S.-led military reign of the country, in April, 1984, Justice Minister Rodrigo Lara, outspoken anti-drug critic, is assassinated. In 1989 the U.S. Secretary of Defense states publicly that finding and eradicating production and transport of drugs is a "high-priority national-security mission" (4). In the same year, Luis Carlos Galan, anti-drug presidential candidate is assassinated. Then, the newly elected president institutes the extradition policy desired by the U.S., militarization of the drug war increases substantially, and the president signs the Decree Law of 1989, "which empowered armed forces to arrest and hold suspects incommunicado for up to seven days in military installations"(5). Throughout this string of events there is a steady increase in militarization and violence. Also clear is that in the midst of the U.S.'s heightened control and influence in the country, it is very dangerous for any member of the Colombian government to be openly against the drug trade or to openly counteract any suggestion from the U.S. government.

The second observable result of the involvement by the U.S. in the region through its security assistance programs is the prevalence of human rights abuses. Specifically, U.S.-trained Latin American military are consistently high human rights abusers. In the words of Jimmy Carter, "The outcome of such training has made Latin American military less humane, less professional, and increasingly focused on civilian (non-military) affairs" (6). In Mexico and Bolivia, the areas where U.S.-sponsored local military anti-drug efforts are greatest, reported human rights violations are also at their highest.

Also a product of the U.S. presence is indiscriminate military expansion and activity, often irrespective of any specific or clear goal. The Colombian government was supplied with twelve Cobra helicopters by the U.S. military, and in the words of author Eugene Bouley, Jr., "the bottom line is that the law permits the use of such weapons only for counter-narcotics operations, but increasingly U.S. representatives, both military and civilian, nod and wink when weapons are used against guerillas and other civilians"(7). Also, in attempts to fight leftist guerillas, U.S.-sponsored militaries often join with drug cartel paramilitary groups in attacking and opposing guerillas. This barrage of military activity can make it extremely difficult to determine actual motives, real progress, and actions which are truly effective. It seems as though hyper-active military presence itself is one of the goals. It is a very effective distraction while also being a mode of implementation of American force to accomplish any desired goal in the region, altruistic or otherwise. It is notable that U.S. sponsored forces intermittently joining with drug cartel forces has apparently not been met with any disapproval by the U.S. in the past several years.

The fourth result of U.S. involvement in the war is that there has been a steady increase in the supply of drugs since the early 1980s, when our presence in Colombia began in earnest. This is ascertainable through CIA and UN estimates of how much money is flowing back to Colombia from the U.S. on an annual basis, which has been fairly consistent or expanding in the past two decades. Further evidence of increased supply is the decrease in the price of cocaine, specifically from

$55,000 per kilo in 1980 to $10,500 per kilo in 1995 (8). This is also the case in Afghanistan. President Karzai and the U.S. Defense Department have repeatedly resisted supporting anti-drug actions in Afghanistan (9). In fact, in 2006, five years after initial U.S. military involvement in the country, the total acreage of poppy fields cultivated (the raw material for opium and heroin production) was 165,000 hectares, the largest heroin crop in recorded history (10). Due to expansion in the southern part of the country, the national crop was even larger in 2007.

In looking at the tangible evidence, there begins to be a clear connection between U.S. involvement and the *promotion,* not the inhibition of the drug trade. These results do not match on any level with the stated goals of the U.S. in this intervention in Latin America. If the casual observer inputs new goals which seem to match more logically with the observable results of our presence in the region, the scene can take on a new clarity. The first of what could be called our "true goals" in Latin America has been to create chaos, destabilization, and war. This creates fear, legitimizes military aggression, and creates a willingness by civilians and government to surrender freedoms in the name of greater perceived safety through heightened military presence. This, as stated above, is precisely what happened inside the borders of the U.S. with the post 9/11 Patriot Act, the quintessence of "Big Brother" vigilance.

The second true goal is expansion of the military and military activity. This allows for control over a populace, gives those in control access to valuable natural resources (drugs or oil), and lets the military monitor money flows in the country. Also, constant and random military activity, aggressive or passive, is very distracting and desensitizes the public to the military, allowing for greater abuses and more intensive involvement. The Afghan national army, for instance, was trained by U.S. military. The Pentagon has also promised to supply the U.S. Drug Enforcement Agency operating in Afghanistan with Mi-17 helicopters but has been slow to deliver (11). Perhaps the DEA's more aggressive drug enforcement approach does not jibe with the Pentagon's larger goals in the area. Also, by 1996, 1,000 Mexican police officers had received special counter-narcotics training in the United States (12).

A third true goal has been the ideological separation between military and the democratic governmental process. This is achieved by keeping a country in a constant state of "emergency" and fear of imminent attack, so that rational constitutional legalities vanish. The military is granted total license to abuse civil and human rights or the environment in order to bring about greater safety. A high level of fear, especially of being attacked or killed by an unseen yet publicly identified force, puts individuals in a primal survival state in which the foundation of a legal, humane society (a constitution or general moral code) is essentially ineffectual. In other words, the population is placed in a state of "no holds barred" and "anything goes" because of their extreme fear. And this is an ideal situation for any military wishing to have access to and control over various societal and economic endeavors.

The fourth mechanism of U.S. involvement is to disguise its motives with a façade of words and actions. This is such a common mechanism of political machines in general, but a few U.S. administrations have employed this more than others. In each case our apparent magnanimity is just a crime, renamed. "Fighting terrorism" = Stealing oil. "Drug War" = Drug cultivation. "Bring them to justice" = Assassinate non-supporters. "Peace-keeping missiles" = Bombs that kill thousands of people.

Fifth is our failure by design. We purposely fail at our stated goal of stopping or diminishing the drug trade, because this allows us to prolong our presence in the region in order to pursue our true goals, which are to cultivate and profit from the drug trade. If it is not by design, then it is quite curious that the most powerful military in the world cannot topple some peasant coca bean farmers and drug gangs with semi-automatic rifles. If we wanted the South American drug war to be over, it would have been so long ago. Similarly, amidst ongoing war in Afghanistan, schools, synagogues, and public services have suffered greatly, yet drug production is thriving. It is widely known that heroin production finances both the Taliban as well as President Karzai's administration, so it is no wonder that drug eradication is proving slow and difficult.

Lastly, America's most sought-after true goal has been to maintain sovereignty over the flow of money in this industry. We do so by constantly shifting our loyalties and alliances in order to take down any powerful individuals or groups in the industry and take over their portion of commerce. We skillfully play government officials and drug czars off each other in order to accomplish this. The U.S. ousts drug czars with the help of government extradition policies, and at the same time condones the assassination of uncooperative politicians with the help of drug czars. One minute a politician or drug leader is our friend, the next they are our hunted foe. This shifting of alliances has been very commonly utilized by our government for decades in myriad global situations. Other former U.S. bed buddies who have since fallen out of favor are Manuel Noriega, Saddam Hussein, Joseph Mobutu of Zaire, and Osama Bin Laden.

There is much evidence showing how the Taliban was supported in the late 90s by the CIA. In his book *Descent into Chaos*, Pakistani journalist Ahmed Rashid states that "Between 1995 and 1996, the USA supported the Taliban politically through its allies in Pakistan and Saudi Arabia, essentially because Washington viewed the Taliban as anti-Iranian, anti-Shia, and pro-Western" (13). British journalist Simon Reeves supports claims that the U.S. supplied Taliban forces with arms and satellite imagery, while author Robert Dreyfuss claims that "U.S. diplomats saw them (the Taliban) as messianic do-gooders -- like born-again Christians from the American Bible Belt" (14). Needless to say, the Taliban has fallen from our good graces in the U.S. and is now perceived as public enemy number one.

After analysis of these true goals, what is occurring yet rarely publicized in drug-producing nations seems very logical: drug income in Colombia has been stabilized and the supply of cocaine has increased, US military presence in Latin America and Afghanistan has been amply secured, and poppy cultivation in Afghanistan has increased dramatically since initial U.S. invasion in 2001 (15).

Amidst all of this drug cultivation as well as efforts at drug suppression in South America, the environment is being substantially damaged. Drug cultivation involves deforestation and subsequent topsoil erosion, pesticide pollution of the soil and surface water, and further pollution through the use of harsh chemicals for drug processing such as sulfuric acid, acetone, and kerosene. The environmental effects of other anti-drug tactics are equally harmful. A chemical defoliant "tebuthiuron," which is so toxic that even its manufacturer, Dow chemical, opposes its use, often renders land unable to grow crops (16). The U.S. embassy, in connection with the host country's minister of the interior, rather than their minister of agriculture, makes decisions on which defoliants to use. This allows for abuses of this nature.

It seems as though America's overarching goal goes even beyond the drug trade, and is simply focused on militarily controlling an entire given region. Now that our military is ensconced in South America for example, and we have secured control and influence over resources, money flows, and governments, we can take advantage economically and politically of virtually any development in this region in the foreseeable future.

In our cultivation of fear to allow public manipulation, and hyper-utilization of the military at home and abroad, the United States at the turn of this century had come to display some classic tendencies of a fascist state. A hyper-aggressive military, censorship of the media, and strong ethnocentrism have been displayed by all major fascist societies of the 20th century. Demonization of an ethnic or racial group – in our most recent case, all Arabs often generally labeled as 'potential terrorists' – is another disturbing sign. Though the Obama administration represents a push away from those tendencies, in some ways, America still operates under this aggressive and myopic national philosophy. The era of excessively male, self-centered, and violent international politics has dominated the globe for millennia, yet in the face of significant social and environmental disasters on the globe today, it is rapidly becoming apparent that this approach no longer serves us as a planet.

The U.S. military's strength has righted many wrongs and brought widespread stability in some critical moments in the past 150 years of global history. Sometimes we go over the line and ignite backlash, however, when military strength turns into military aggression and imperialism.

The change of leadership philosophy as well as the financial crisis, both in early 2009, have served to turn some of our attention and money from war onto issues back at home. President Obama, whether supported or denounced, has espoused a much more open, communicative, and inclusive approach to managing the United States of America. Some see this approach as weak, yet I see it as strong, necessary, and of increasing effectiveness. The $787 billion stimulus package, successful though not unilaterally praised, is focused domestically, investing in education, building transportation and electric infrastructure, developing solar and wind technologies, and fostering true diplomacy. This bodes well for our future.

More broadly, any discussion of the international drug trade must look at individual consumption of drugs as part of the problem. That is where residents of wealthy drug-consuming nations, such as the U.S, Western Europe and Japan, can be a small part of the solution. It can be unsettling and also tempting to ignore one pertinent and simple truth; our personal choices have more power than we think they do. Irresponsible consumption in industrialized nations is at the root of many local and global problems, and the surprisingly voluminous usage of drugs is no different. We must begin to perceive the global implications of our choices and see that the decisions of what to eat, what energy to vote for and use, and even whether or not we use illegal drugs have global-scale ramifications.

Dependence on Oil

The Fostering of Demand, an Apparently Limitless Supply by Design, and the Insidious Suppression of Environmental Truths and Awareness

In the summer of 2008 I was flying from Houston to Los Angeles next to an oil industry engineer and salesman who I found to be quite glib. We spoke at length about oil, coal, and natural gas, but it was difficult to get more than a few words out of him when the topic of renewable energy came up.

"I know oil reservoirs are drying up pretty quickly," I said to him, gauging his response. "When your best sites start to run out of oil, you could probably make a lot of money tapping solar or wind power on those exact same sites."

"Maybe," he said, "but we're not tooled for that. We're tooled for oil. When sites dry up, we just search farther and dig deeper."

His unwavering focus – well, fixation -- on oil actually surprised me. How could he or his company be so adamantly centered on one source of energy, with all of its inherent problems, when there are other energy sources at their finger tips that are vastly more cost-effective and cause no environmental harm? But then I realized that this describes much of the world: blindly dependent on oil to the bitter end.

Dependence on oil is a very powerful and astonishingly pervasive tool. Those who control the resource of oil – a conglomerate coupling oil companies and several U.S. governmental administrations – utilize this dependence very effectively to ensure their continued wealth and dominance. Dependence on oil is generated through several specific mechanisms, including: ensuring ample supply, fostering demand and consumption, suppressing awareness of environmental crises, and sabotaging renewable energy information and industrial ventures. The engendering of this dependence among oil powers and Western political elites is sourced in attitudes of greed for disproportionate wealth at the expense of others, and a myopic disregard for the planet's environment.

Their most essential mechanism is securing an ample supply of oil. The apparent goal is to create a carefree feeling among the American populace, the greatest oil market in the world, so that consumption will never be restricted. It should be said that a government going to lengths to care for the needs of its citizens is a worthy endeavor. The two presidential administrations of George W. Bush showed themselves to be efficacious, powerful, and single-minded about their acquisition of oil to supply our domestic demand. They "got the job done," as it were, by any means necessary. That kind of effectiveness is critical to the functioning of a government. Neither worthy nor necessary, however, was the active cultivation of excessive consumption of this environmentally harmful product, as well as the consistent suppression of its superior alternatives.

This fixation extends to staunch support of coal, natural gas, and nuclear power as purportedly critical energy sources for our future. These are all controllable finite resources, and therefore they provide excellent opportunities for monopolization and profit. Hence, powerful government lobbies fight tooth and nail against lowering carbon emissions and tightening environmental standards because environmentalism lowers profits for these deleterious industries and removes the fabricated competitive edge that they now enjoy. Coal is the most polluting of all energy sources, yet it still provides close to 30% of the world's energy. Natural gas burns cleaner than coal per unit of energy produced, but it nonetheless generates significant amounts of CO_2 and its extraction process commonly pollutes local groundwater stores. Besides producing copious radioactive waste, nuclear power plants require more water than any other modern energy source in order to function properly. It is difficult to monopolize the sun or the wind, so solar and wind power are not as attractive as income sources for those who currently monopolize fossil fuels and nuclear power.

A few historical twists favored the adoption of oil. During World War II, oil was essential to the functioning of armies on both sides, and oil embargoes against Axis powers were critical to their defeat. The United States realized the importance of a steady supply of oil to its livelihood. To that end, the U.S. took two landmark geopolitical actions. Immediately following World War II, the Bretton Woods agreement was signed in New Hampshire in 1944, which established the International Monetary Fund and the World Bank (1). Located inside the United States, these institutions use their considerable financial leverage to grant Western businesses access to third-world economies and resources. Then, in 1945, President Franklin D. Roosevelt met with Kind Abdul Asiz Ibn Saud of Saudi Arabia to set up an oil-for-protection arrangement that is still the foundation of the U.S./ Saudi relationship (2). These two mechanisms were powerful assurance of the future access to and availability of oil for the U.S.

Today, the pressure to discover new sources of oil is much greater. According to the U.S. Energy Information Administration, between 2000 and 2020, U.S. oil production will fall from over 7 million barrels per day to under 5 million barrels per day, yet consumption will increase from 15 million barrels per day to well over 22 million barrels per day. Therefore, by 2020, the US will need to import twice as much fuel per year as it did in 2000. In order to perpetuate the idea of limitless supply of oil in the first decade of this century, the Bush government faced the task of actively and aggressively acquiring larger and more varied sources of oil. Our most common and effective means for achieving this has been military invasion.

In the year 2000, an oil pipeline had been conceived of to pass from the oil-rich Caspian Sea, through Afghanistan, and to the ports of Pakistan for transport. Yet the Taliban leadership of Afghanistan, former associates of the Bush Sr. administration, were not amenable to this pipeline plan. Also, Iraq's third largest oil reserves on Earth were despotically guarded by Saddam Hussein, a former operative of the CIA, which was headed by Bush Sr. at the time. These were identified as huge potential new sources of petroleum, and all that was need was an "entrance strategy" into these countries.

A few months before September 11, 2001, a briefing to Dick Cheney and George Bush read:

"Based on a review of all sources reporting over the last five months, we believe that UBL will launch a significant terrorist attack against the U.S. and/or Israel's interests in the coming weeks. The attack will be spectacular and designed to inflict mass casualties against U.S. facilities or interests. Attack preparations have been made. Attack will occur with little or no warning" (3).

Two months later 9/11 occurred, and soon after, the U.S. military entered Afghanistan, and several events immediately ensued which had nothing to do with terrorism and everything to do with oil acquisition in the Caspian region. First, the Pakistani oil minister met with former U.S. ambassador to Pakistan, Wendy Chamberlin, about a proposed pipeline from the Caspian Sea to Pakistan. This pipeline passed through Afghanistan. Then, Taliban-occupied Kabul fell to U.S. military. In December, the new Afghan president, Hamid Karzai, was sworn in and received $50 million from the White House and $100 million from the IMF for the construction of a pipeline maintenance road. Soon after, Karzai spoke with Pakistani officials about putting the pipeline into effect. Mission oil acquisition in Afghanistan accomplished. The next target was Iraq.

Having its sights set on Iraq's oil for some time, the Bush/Cheney team had been attempting to link Iraq to 9/11 for several months, and to justify a future invasion. On November 8, 2002, Resolution 1441 was passed by the UN Security Council which stated that "Iraq will face serious consequences (since they have not) provided an accurate, full, final, and complete disclosure . . . of all aspects of its progress to develop weapons of mass destruction" (4). This resolution was spearheaded and heavily backed by the U.S. and the U.K. Then, several comments by White House officials began to link 9/11 to Iraq, including a statement by Dick Cheney on National Public Radio in January, 2003: "There's overwhelming evidence (that) there was a connection between Al Qaeda and the Iraq government" (5).

No such evidence was ever provided. If any more clarification was needed on the White House's intentions concerning this matter, they were disclosed by the final report of the National Commission on Terrorist Attacks on the United States, also known as the 9/11 Commission. It stated that specific members of the Bush administration deliberately used 9/11 as justification to invade Iraq (6). 9/11 was a terrible tragedy in the history of our nation's people, yet interestingly, it proved to be quite helpful to the oil oligarchy's continuing quest to secure new sources of its commodity.

Waging war is, unfortunately, far from the end of the desperate measures to which oil/government conglomerates go in order to acquire more oil. In the words of Matt Elmer, operations manager for Conoco Phillips, "There's not a lot of easy oil left to be found, otherwise we would have found it… Right now we are pushing out to more remote areas, pushing out to deeper waters, whether it's the Gulf of Mexico or offshore Alaska" (7). The "oil sands" of Alberta, Canada is a region where companies are literally bull-dozing trees in order to excavate oil-saturated soil and squeeze every last drop from it. In the great central valley of California, Chevron has already extracted most of the "sweet" crude oil and now all that is left is denser, thicker petroleum which is too viscous to be pumped to the surface. Rather than just looking upwards and capturing the abundant sunshine and wind in California with panels and turbines, the oil giant is plunging super-heated steam into these deep wells in order to soften the oil enough to remove it. According to the National Geographic Channel, this requires 81 trillion BTUs of energy every day, which is enough to power an air conditioner for every person on Earth (8). Clearly this process is requiring more energy than it is producing, which manifests the inherent desperation and lack of economic and environmental logic.

Companies such as British Petroleum are drilling farther and farther offshore in ever-deeper waters, which is proving to be disastrously uncontrollable. In April of 2010, some fifty miles off the coast of New Orleans, a mile-deep well ruptured and began to spew millions of gallons of oil per day. It took BP three months to cap the geyser, but not before 200 million gallons of oil were released, making it one of the largest spills in global history. The leak has severely degraded the regional ecosystem and the fishing economy of the Gulf States. As a comparison, there are no catastrophic spills of wind or sunshine, nor are there any significant negative effects on the environment from renewables such as solar, wind, wave, or geothermal energy.

Another mechanism used by the oil power oligarchy to ensure dependence on oil is the suppression of awareness of the current global environment crisis. If the public knew how devastating this oil consumption was to the environment, and the insidious lengths to which the U.S. government has gone in order to secure it, massive changes would occur in consumption of oil and in the public perception of various presidential administrations. Perhaps as a result, several presidential administrations have displayed remarkable political skill in non-disclosure and bending of obvious truths related to oil.

To begin, due to myriad factors including a devotion to "journalistic balance," difficulty deciphering confusing scientific jargon, and covert pressure from oil powers, U.S. media has become a virtual accomplice to oil industry public relations groups in suppressing the connection between fossil fuel burning and global warming (9). "We did make the link to global warming once," said one TV news editor, "but it triggered a barrage of complaints from the Global Climate Coalition to our top network executives" (The GCC was the oil and coal lobbying group) (10). The absence of this link to global warming leaves a critical gap which is elucidated by authors Maxwell and Jules Bykoff:

"Since the general public garners most of its knowledge about science from the mass media . . . the disjuncture between scientific discourse and popular discourse (is responsible for the fact that) significant and concerted international action has not been taken to curb practices that contribute to global warming" (11).

This suppression goes past the media and into the realm of government. According to the EPA, in 2003, the agency's report on the environmental effects of climate change on the

U.S. had four paragraphs removed after the White House had access to it (12). Also, by 2003, ExxonMobil was giving more than one million dollars a year to an array of ideological, right-wing organizations opposing action on climate change, including the Competitive Enterprise Institute, and Frontiers of Freedom (13).

Beyond subterfuge and hiding of the facts, there is also simple open denouncement of environmentalism and conservation. At an Associated Press meeting in Toronto in April of 2001, Dick Cheney belittled the suggestion that "we could simply conserve or ration our way out" of an energy crisis. "Conservation may be a sign of personal virtue, but it is not a sufficient basis for a sound comprehensive energy policy" (14).

These are only glimpses of the suppression of environmental awareness by the government and media. When necessary, suppression of facts is utilized, but on the global scale, a brash indifference to the environment in general is the tool. For example, in the late 90s Holland, Germany, and Britain agreed to cut their emissions by 50 to 80 percent over the next fifty years, and China has cut emissions by 19 percent even while showing 36 percent economic growth over the same period (15). During this same span of time, the U.S. offered a significantly smaller reduction in emissions than its European counter parts and also twice pulled out of the Kyoto environmental protocols (16). The undying support of fossil fuels that U.S. governmental policy and legislation exhibited for decades has produced insidious, deleterious, and pervasive environmental damage. The power of this greed has produced a myopia that simply does not allow for the acknowledgement that the effects of this oil oligarchy's actions are threatening the very survival of the human race. Only with an intense myopia could this barrage of environmentally harmful practices continue.

In addition to the suppression of information about

climate change, there is also active sabotage over the last fifty years of solar and alternative transport technology by the oil powers. Solar technology companies that show any potential for success are often bought out by no-name businesses and then totally shut down. It seems unlikely that this would happen so often, since there would be no economic incentive, if it were not the oil powers behind these actions. Also, in the late 1950s in the Los Angeles metropolitan area, a conglomerate of General Motors, Standard Oil, and Firestone Tires bought out the city's largest electric light-rail system. Named the Pacific Electric, this was an incredibly extensive network of railways stretching sixty miles inland and along approximately seventy miles of urban development on the coast. It was bought out and totally dismantled by 1961, and the largest urban car center on the planet was born. There are now fifteen million cars in Southern California, which is more than the total in any foreign country. A very similar buyout and dismantling of public transportation systems occurred in approximately sixty other U.S. cities.

Moreover, in the late 1990s, General Motors produced an all-electric car, the EV-1, under mandate from the state of California. Despite a large demand, GM did not allow purchase of the cars, only leasing. After the mandate was no longer in effect, GM recalled every single EV-1, then crushed and shredded them at a facility in Arizona. This is documented in the film "Who Killed the Electric Car?" and discussed more at length in the "Living Efficiently" chapter in this book. Suffice it to say that alternatives to fossil fuels and to fossil fuel-based transport have not exactly been given an equal chance.

Solar power, for instance, is often described as "too expensive" and "impractical" by oil industry spokespeople. Yet some simple facts discredit this. Solar has a one-time set up cost, it is emission free, there is little required maintenance on solar-receiving apparatus, sunshine is virtually ubiquitous, and there is a limitless supply of solar energy for the next

five billion years (until the sun runs out of hydrogen to burn).
Moreover, no one goes to war over solar or wind power. A
fortuitous sign of solar power's imminent wide acceptance is
that just before the signing of the economic stimulus package
of 2009, the owner of a solar power company in Colorado was
chosen to introduce President Obama.

Finding oil, on the contrary, is very expensive and
requires satellite imagery, magnetic resonance technology,
and much manpower. Drilling apparatus and operation is
financially and energetically costly, as is environmental clean
up from frequent spillages in transport. You may be aware
of the infamous Exxon Valdez oil tanker crash of 1989 in
which 10 million gallons of oil were spilled along the coast
of Alaska. The event caused a massive public outcry and
garnered publicity worldwide. That said, it may be surprising
to know that thirty-three even larger oil spills occurred before
the Exxon Valdez, and there have been fifteen larger spills in
the years since (17). Some of the notably large spills were the
following: 1979 Atlantic Empress – 77 million gallons, 1983
Castillo de Bellver – 68 million gallons, 1991 ADT Summer
– 70 million gallons, and in 1991 Saddam Hussein ordered
several tankers to release 520 million gallons of oil into the
Persian Gulf in order to slow the U.S. military invasion (18).
This is a catastrophic amount of oil spilled into the ocean
ecological systems over the past few decades and yet this
topic is conspicuously, and consistently, absent from news
programming.

The final mechanism to be discussed is the fostering of
demand. First, preceding the Obama administration, there was
rarely a mention of "conservation" in any public government
statement. It is not that it was denounced, but rather that it was
almost never mentioned. Conservation is the biggest enemy
of the commercial oil machine, while ignorant, unmitigated
consumption is its greatest accomplice.

In the last fifty years, in fact, conservation has been

essentially absent from the American modus operandi. Consumption has become part of the foundational ethos of this country through the growth of capitalism and advertising. Omnipresent automobile ads and a proliferation of gas-guzzling SUVs are testament to our unbridled enjoyment of and carefree indulgence in the delights of fossil fuels. There is a powerful affinity between the American identity and our automobiles. This is one of the greatest marketing tools for oil consumption, because while we are focused on how our car uniquely expresses who we are, those who profit from oil have already won their victory in that we are driving at all.

This perception of a limitless supply of oil is visually represented by the stunning prevalence of gasoline stations in every urban area in the United States. Gas stations are located on the corners of nearly every principle intersection in modern American cities. Their vast horizontal space for pulling out of the hubbub of urban driving is a tantalizing oasis in dense urban areas. With the advent of AM/PM mini-markets, which are often open twenty-four hours, gas stations now provide not only gasoline, but food, public phones, restrooms, and even basic household supplies. Myriad car ads marketing the automobile as the ultimate visceral and voyeuristic expression of our identity, and the instilling of an unquenchable desire for ever-increasing horsepower, have made unbridled fossil fuel consumption in this culture a given.

In summation, the current oil oligarchy, which combines oil industry and government players, goes to great lengths to ensure an ample supply of oil, to foster its demand, and to downplay the link between fossil fuel burning and global warming. New, clean, renewable energy technologies have also been actively suppressed for decades. The result, very simply, is that the United States and much of the globe is dependent on oil and fossil fuels, by design.

SOLUTIONS

A Rising Tide Lifts All Boats

"[Disease], hunger and food insecurity are injustices, with national and international institutions and actors significantly responsible. In other words, they are largely preventable and solvable problems, if human will is there to resolve them."

- Author Alison Symington, *Defending our Dreams*, 2005

A dear friend of mine from El Salvador once told me that in the poor villages and towns of her country, most families do not have enough money to take their sick children to the doctor or even to buy basic medicines. Small health problems such as fevers or infections can quickly become life-threatening. Without the option of medical care, when a child becomes ill the most common response is simply to gather neighbors together and pray long into the night.

Contemplating the plight of those villagers, and millions of others like them, left me speechless. No one should have to endure illness and emotional anguish that could have been avoided with a medicine that costs only a dollar or two. An immense amount of suffering in our midst can be assuaged by a tiny amount of attention and money. Maybe you, holding this book right now, will be the answer to the next prayer that cries out to the world from a small neighborhood in El

Salvador. Perhaps you will decide to donate just $25 or $50 to an organization that helps provide medical care and food in that region. And maybe that gift will end up saving a life, or ten lives, or feeding an entire family for a month.

The compassion that I trust you feel in your heart right now is the most important ingredient in our present and future success as a planet. There is a growing wave of positive energy which is uplifting and healing the world which is comprised of the attitudes of love, compassion, and awareness. This energy takes on many forms and expressions throughout the world, and it is, of course, expanding all the time. Part of this wave of benevolent energy is sourced in the first, or industrialized, world because a large portion of its population has achieved effortless subsistence and is able to shift its attention to global-scale altruistic purposes. Many corporate and political leaders throughout the world increasingly display tenets of this positive wave, as well. Many U.S. presidential administrations, most recently those of Nixon, Carter, Clinton, and Obama have often shown the intention to be a part of this trend.

The two main avenues of this love and compassion are short and long-term aid to the third world and the healing of the environment. Yet before these two avenues could become significant global forces, they were necessarily preceded by a raised global awareness. This expanded awareness, which is the foundation of the current tide of benevolence on Earth, is based on the evolution and improvement of technology. The internet, cell phones, and twenty-four hour global news (CNN and BBC) have allowed us to be instantly connected to each other and to information all the time through virtually any medium. This instantly brought light to dark corners of the globe which made local injustices global issues. The globalization of culture – largely through American and Western music, television, movies, and fast food – with debatable pros and cons, has had the effect of creating a feeling of connectedness while fortifying English as the universal language. Finally, jet air travel, albeit a less recent technological innovation, has generated the world-changing possibility of traveling around the world in a matter of hours. Loved ones can be reached, wars can be photographically documented, and environmental catastrophes can instantly be videoed and analyzed. This, again, had an immediate effect on our awareness of each other.

The increased knowledge of the world spurred individuals, organizations, and governments to offer help to the newly identified regions of need. Wealthy and international philanthropists such as Ted Turner, Oprah Winfrey, Bono, Bill Gates, and Richard Branson have set a precedent for private benevolence with altruistic agendas that go beyond and offer a broader spectrum of help than traditional governmental aid. Non-governmental organizations such as Amnesty International, UNICEF, Habitat for Humanity, the Red Cross, World Vision, Greenpeace, Britain's OXFAM, and literally thousands of others have taken it upon themselves to move the globe in a new direction and show compassion, sometimes even in the face of much resistance. The United Nations is undeniably the most important benevolent organization on the planet whose effects of nuclear disarmament, peace-keeping, and human rights assurance are changing the course of global societal evolution. Many nations in Europe offer support for the environment and are joined by the United States in their international protection of human rights.

The destinations of this personal and institutional philanthropy are short and long-term aid to the developing world and the amelioration of the Earth's environment. Short-term aid is essentially food, housing, medical care and disaster relief for the most beleaguered regions and nations. This voluminous and ongoing relief helps to feed almost one billion undernourished people and provide shelter for the several hundred million with inadequate housing. The complement to immediate relief is aid geared towards long-term recovery, redevelopment, and social equality. This includes programs such as organic farming, education and start-up capital for various projects, establishing clean water supplies, financing infrastructure development such as highways and railroads, and setting up domestic human rights abuse-monitoring organizations. Long-term assistance is provided by several well-known organizations contracted by the United Nations to provide localized assistance.

Nature itself is the other main recipient of this love and aid. Organizations such as the Sierra Club, Greenpeace, The Nature Conservancy, and the World Wildlife Fund have been protecting the environment and animals for several decades. They promote environmental causes on both the local and global scale – from protecting a single tract of land to lobbying governments to sign international pollution reduction agreements. Their modus operandi, equally broad, includes grassroots volunteerism, regional environmental education promotion, and international advertising campaigns. Individual philanthropists have also had an impact on the environment. Ted Turner is a true environmentalist, donating hundreds of millions to environmental efforts in his lifetime. Richard Branson, owner of Virgin Airways, has pledged three billion dollars of his company's profits to help fight global warming.

Third-world women as a group are another salient destination for altruism. Uplifting women is a theme throughout this book, and it must become a broad effort that knows no socioeconomic or national boundaries. To say that women are oppressed is a huge understatement. At least one out of every three women around the world has been beaten, coerced into sex, or otherwise abused in her lifetime (1). Moreover, domestic violence causes more death and disability worldwide amongst women aged 15-44 than war, cancer, malaria, and traffic accidents combined (2). I am shocked each time I read these statistics, and so we must continually repeat, reinforce, and refresh our efforts to improve the lives of women everywhere. We can do this in our personal lives with small decisions every day, and also we can support organizations that fight for women legislatively, politically, and socially. Several of these organizations are listed in the introduction to this book. A few more are "Womankind Worldwide" and "Pro Mujer." Also, http://www.delicateforest.com is a website that sells products made by formerly trafficked and exploited women and children.

Broadly, short-term and long-term aid to third world economies and people are having the combined effect of allowing inhabitants and nations to get back on their feet, as it were. With their immediate needs met, developing world denizens and organizations can invest themselves in collaborative projects with aid organizations such as sustainable agriculture, infrastructure building, and economic development and industrialization aimed at an earnest participation in the global economy. These ameliatory trends are fortifying these nations and helping to curb the massive flow of millions of people from the over-burdened countryside to cities in search of food and jobs. Examples of such cities that were already discussed are Sao Paolo, Mumbai, and Mexico City. Each has over twenty million inhabitants. Industrialized development also encourages a reduction in birth rates, while an assurance of basic human rights has positive effects on all levels of society.

When these poorer nations become more self-sustaining, healthy and productive societies, then they can finally begin to give to the world their true gifts, their unique contribution to the global, cultural, and economic potpourri. With most of the population of the globe now living in the so-called "developing world," the latent potential for cultural expansion and development is awesome. When these nations more fully step into themselves and into their role in this new age, then an egalitarian mutual uplifting can occur with the rest of the world. For instance, a focus on family sanctity, community-based identity and problem solving, and awareness of nature can be communicated from the developing world to the developed world where more of a return to this foundation is needed. In this way, less developed nations can serve as the "roots" of global society, while the technology, democracy, and social awareness of the first world can be the "wings." Yet these traditional roles will dissolve as equal exchange and mutual acknowledgment increases.

As the suffering and overlooked injustices of the developing world are brought to the light of day, and as these nations rise and express their true potential, they will display and fulfill their part of the evolving global cultural mosaic. In addition, first world denizens can continue to step out of complacency and into an active role in solving global-scale problems. Likewise, as the globe becomes increasingly involved in the protection of its environment, governments and corporations will begin to broaden their goals beyond immediate profit to the greater good of humanity and long-term harmony with nature.

From this new perspective comes the realization that we are all a part of the same larger whole, an amalgam of diverse cultures in a living relationship and symbiosis with the Earth as our home. An acceptance and reverence for each other and for the Earth naturally ensues. And the final stage of this beautiful expansion of benevolence on the globe is a feeling of love and acceptance for every human, by every human, and a conscious collective decision to remain in a state of appreciation and harmony with the Earth.

An experience that I had many years ago while traveling in Southeast Asia may be a fitting end to this chapter about planetary solutions and mutual uplifting. I had been traveling for a few days with two Brits named Roger and Nigel when we found ourselves on Tioman Island, just northeast of Singapore in the South China Sea. Upon arrival at the large, mountainous island covered in thick jungle, it was clear that it had been only minimally developed for local residence or

(continued after photo insert)

Standing with my buddy, Neil (to my left), by a melting glacier near the Matterhorn in Switzerland, 1990.

Marveling at the assortment of fruit in Vietnam, 1999.

A swarm of camera-friendly Thai school kids and I in Bangkok, 1998.

Rest stop on a group hike in mountains outside of Chiang Mai, Thailand, 1998.

At the end of a rainbow in a remote village in Thailand's Golden Triangle, 1999.

A traveling Brit and I having breakfast in Bangkok, 1999.

Trekking through Thailand by elephant, 1999.

Tight quarters: a $3 hotel room 5'x 7' in Kuala Lumpur, Malaysia, 1998.

Waiting for a boat to Koh Samui, a spectacularly beautiful island in southern Thailand, 1998.

My friend "Mon" selling her wares to tourists on Phuket island, Thailand, 1998.

My sister and I in Cairo, 1999.

I was assured by the Masai tribesman we camped with that the red cloak protected me from lions! Kenya, 1996.

On safari in Kenya's Masai Mara game reserve, 1996.

In a recently deforested section of Costa Rica, translating for North American man on business trip, 1995.

Tired but exhilarated, hiking through Costa Rican rainforest, 1995.

Standing at 16,500 feet on a volcano in the Andes Mountains, 1996.

Witnessing global warming first-hand at a snowless Argentine ski resort in mid-winter, 1996.

Altiplano near Chile-Bolivia border with llamas in background, 1996.

With students
volunteering
at Tierra
Miguel
organic
farm near
Temecula,
CA, 2008.

Weeding with
students at
Tierra Miguel
farm, 2009.

Gathering
food at Tierra
Miguel farm,
2010.

Talking to Frederick Ndabaramiye, Rwandan genocide survivor, after he spoke to my class at Cal State Northridge, 2010.

Me (center) and one of my favorite classes at Cal State University Northridge, 2008.

tourism in any way. It was truly a place that was away from it all. The owner of the small structure near the beach where we were staying mentioned that there was a hotel and a restaurant on the other side of the island. The only way to get there was to wait for the bi-weekly ferry boat or to hike over a jungle-covered ridge of hills and down to the other side of the island. Zealous and young, we opted to take the challenging hike which the owner said would take "a few hours."

We set out the next morning without packs or supplies, thinking we would buy whatever we needed once we arrived at the hotel, likely by noon. Hiking uphill, through jungle, and in the tropical sun and humidity proved a bit more of a challenge than we had anticipated. Two hours into the hike, we still had not even reached the crest of the hills which we would then need to descend on the other side. Our intermittent chatter progressively grew silent as we could sense the growing danger that we were lost, battling oppressive elements, and on an island that was essentially uninhabited. And being lost in the jungle is not like any other experience of being lost. You can walk literally thirty feet, then turn around and have no visual clues as to where you just came from. As time passed, I began to imagine what creatures would be roaming this jungle when night fell and how we would defend ourselves. Just as the sensation of fear had most certainly overtaken the feeling of adventure on this sojourn, we came into a small clearing and what we saw changed everything.

In front of us were a man, whom we later found out to be Dutch, and his son daintily pulling nets through the air in attempts to capture and photograph butterflies. Roger, Nigel, and I all stopped – profusely sweating and exhausted – and stared at the two naturalists incredulously. Even before any words were exchanged, I immediately felt the stress drain from my body, based simply on the fact that this father and son clearly perceived there to be no danger nor cause for worry due to our isolated location. I finally spoke and asked the man if he had any idea how to get back to civilization.

"I know exactly where we are," the man responded. "I know this island like my own backyard!" Gesturing, though keeping his eyes trained on a butterfly, he said "Just keep going in that direction over the crest of the hill and you'll hit the beach in a few miles. Then follow the beach north until you see the hotel."

His superior awareness of the island and his calm *knowing* that everything was going to be all right made our worries vanish instantly. About an hour later, we arrived at the hotel, safe and sound. What stayed with me from that encounter was how profoundly one person's experience and peaceful attitude can transform all of the people around him. It showed me the power of knowledge and deep awareness in times of crisis or fear. And many places on the planet, each in different ways, are experiencing crises or chaos right now. Armed with some rudimentary wisdom of global issues, and how to begin to solve them, each one of us can become that knowledgeable, calming entity that conciliates and transforms those around them. With this expanded and informed perspective, we can each be a guide to others and a presence that lets them know that even in trying times, everything is going to be all right.

A Beacon of Light

"O beautiful for glory-tale
Of liberating strife
When once and twice,
for man's avail
Men lavished precious life!
America! America!"

- *America the Beautiful,* lyrics by
Katharine Lee Bates

On a dusty road between two rural villages near the Masai Mara game reserve in Kenya, I came across a man selling beautiful batik wall hangings. They were adorned with scenes of Masai tribal life and I was very intrigued, so I asked him "How much?" He immediately began inspecting the clothes and travel gear that I was wearing.

"I like Nike," he said in a thick accent. I shook my head because I wasn't going to part with my most comfortable shoes. Taking a peek at the tag on my shirt he said,

"Calvin Klein! …how many do you have?"

As simple as that, a deal was brokered: one extravagant four-foot by six-foot tribal batik in exchange for three white Calvin Klein T-shirts. I came to realize on that trip and on subsequent overseas journeys that American goods and

American culture are known and desired in every corner of the globe. The U.S. has its shortcomings – a discussion of which has not been avoided in this book – but the culture and ethos of the United States is unique and certainly the most recognized on the planet.

Our spirit of ambition, innovation, and our ability to think big are continually changing global realities and expanding notions of what is possible. In a world full of rich traditions and cultures that have developed over centuries, what is proffered by the U.S. -- a mere babe of 200-some years -- is a fresh, uplifting experiment in casting history aside and creating the future with inspired abandon. American culture vibrates with excitement and greatness and bursts with abundance, self-expression and radiance. These feelings are an expression of the desire that all human beings share to be bigger and to be *more*, and so our nation seems to elicit the most intrigue and attraction around the globe. Our products are tangible representations of this energy and lifestyle, and the world cannot get enough of them. Our Nikes, Levis, Coca Cola, and MTV let people purchase or consume a tiny piece of American life.

Our movies, television programs and music broadcast our way of life to the world. Our movies, in particular, help the world to dream. They transport millions of people from daily mundane struggles and show a better life and an exciting or dynamic existence, however contrived it may be. In this way, American celebrities become the world's icons, and what these celebrities wear and drink and talk about instantly become desired commodities.

Everyone wants to feel exceptional, special, and grand. But perhaps even more, people all over the world want to feel *cool*. And there is no cooler place than "the States." The U.S. shows us that when we risk greatly and trust in ourselves, anything is possible.

This is not to say that this nation is devoid of problems.

We are not perfect – certainly imperialistic, perhaps avaricious, a bit oblivious to the rest of the world, and to varying degrees, wasteful. Yet what is *good* about this country is indispensable and invaluable. This nation is the football star who's also an A student. He's got a nice car and likes to party a bit too much but everybody wants to be around him. Deep down he has a good heart, but most attractive of all – he's got a bright future. And that's all anyone or any country wants to know: that the future looks bright and much good is on the way. For this reason, the United States is truly a great country.

And sometimes, when you are uninspired or downtrodden or taught that you are less, or you've been suppressed by thought and physical control and limitation for so long – it is challenging to see the greatness in yourself. So it can be helpful to first see the greatness in another. This is uplifting because it is proof that greatness does indeed exist, which is a major leap of perspective to one who is truly downtrodden. When one sees this greatness in another, it finally seems possible. By experiencing American movies and products and national passion, others get a glimpse of success, and this can spur them to envision their own success. This boost, even though from without, engages something deep within. The parts of a person that are naturally vibrating at this level move, stir, and come alive. When these feelings of magnificence within them are expressed, they are a unique and beautiful gift to the world. These gifts are something that cannot be found anywhere else on the planet. When all worlds, all nations, all cultures, and all individuals start to engage their own magnificence, the bounty and abundance and diverse richness of extraordinary creations will pour forth. We will be reminded of how much latent potential that this globe possesses.

Italian cars, French food and wine, Costa Rican environmentalism, Swiss banks and watches, Thai hospitality, Japanese precision, Brazilian sensuality, African community

and resilience, Chinese stability, and American ingenuity –
these are all unique offerings. There is no equivalent to German
organization, Rwandan buoyancy, Singaporean cleanliness,
and Jamaican vibrancy. And when you produce what you are
best at, you do it abundantly and with joy, and you will receive
abundance in return. Eventually, we will need fewer artificial
exchanges mediated by money, because goods and services
will be created not for profit, but for the joy of creating them.
We will be blessed and supported by the unique creations
and offerings of others, and they will be supported by ours. A
farmer cannot eat all of his apples, so he provides them for the
community. A teacher requires students in order to share her
gifts, and a doctor has no purpose without people in need of
healing. Giving and receiving are a part of the same whole and
because of this, all needs are naturally met. This is our destiny
as a planet and it is not too far away.

The First Way to Save the Planet

Convert to Solar: Solar power is inexpensive, ubiquitous, produces no pollution, and it never runs out. In the next fifty years, it will transform the global economy, the environment, and it will dramatically enhance U.S. national security. Adoption of solar power and other renewables, such as wind power, on a large scale means replacing coal as the main producer of our electricity. This saves millions of tons of CO_2 from going into our atmosphere every year. This one shift, therefore, may be the single most powerful act to diminish global warming that the industrialized world can make. A change to renewable energy will also translate to drastically reduced dependence on foreign sources of energy, such as oil. This means less money spent on wars and military activity and less provoking of terrorist retaliation. Some companies now install solar panels at no up-front cost, and you can also vote for solar power to be implemented in your city, state, and nation.

Solar Energy

*"The ice caps wouldn't be melting, and neither would I...
energy would fall right down from the sky... that's my dream
world."*

**- "Dreamworld" (2009) by Robin Thicke,
Grammy Award-Winning R&B Singer**

*"Solar power is the biggest business opportunity the world has
ever seen."*

**- Ted Turner, billionaire, philanthropist and creator
of CNN, the first 24-hour news network (1)**

Providing energy to the world made John D. Rockefeller III
and J. Paul Getty two of the richest men the world has ever
known. More recent oil magnates dot the landscape in the
Middle East, central Asia, and the United States. In the 21st
century, self-made billionaires will also provide energy for the
world, but now it will come from the sun. As evidence of this,
Shi Zhengrong, creator of Suntech, a solar cell manufacturer, is
already China's second wealthiest man (2).

     The Earth's consumption of energy will escalate by
nearly 40% in the next twenty years, and most of that will be

fueled by dwindling fossil fuel supplies, causing an unwieldy rise in electricity costs (3). The inevitable switch to unlimited, cheap, and non-polluting alternative energies is already occurring, and solar power is the fastest growing energy source on the planet. During his State of the Union address in January of 2010, President Obama stated, "The nation that leads the clean-energy economy is the nation that will lead the global economy. The United States must be that nation."

The change over to solar power is occurring at the national, community, and individual scales. Home owners who don't utilize solar power are likely already paying too much for energy, and this will only be magnified in the next several years. Solar City is the largest residential supplier of solar power in the U.S. and it serves over 500 communities in Arizona, California, Colorado, Oregon, and Texas. This company is one of several which are making the dream of a solar-powered world into a reality. Many U.S. solar companies will now install photovoltaic solar panels on a home at no upfront cost and craft payments to be smaller than the household's current monthly electricity bill. That is, homeowners can now switch to clean solar power and save money instantly. Moreover, as electricity costs skyrocket and most residents are subject to the utility company's price whims, solar homes will be producing their own energy right at home: off the grid, emission-free and independent of any market or government agency. On the political spectrum, that's the Democratic *and* the Republican ideal all in one. Solar power and other renewables have arrived and are here to stay.

Throughout history the world has satisfied its energy needs through a wide array of sources: wind power for ocean voyages, animal power for agriculture and transportation, and the heat of the sun to warm us and allow plants to grow. Within the past two centuries, the globe has developed an addiction to a new form of energy – the burning of fossil fuels in the form of coal, petroleum, and natural gas. The result is that we are experiencing massive environmental degradation due to global warming, pollution, large-scale wars waged over oil, and a monopolization of global wealth and energy by only a few Western companies. These potent yet very problematic fossil fuels have served our needs for some time, but for hundreds and even thousands of years, a better, cleaner, and limitless form of energy has been ever present – the energy of the sun.

In the words of author Frank Kryza, "Harnessing the sun's energy is one of human kind's oldest fantasies, ranking with perpetual motion and the transmutation of base metals into gold" (4). The ancient Greek academician and engineer Archimedes set fire to enemy ships with the reflected light of the sun. Leonardo da Vinci proposed the idea of solar power being used for commercial purposes. In the late 19th century, inventor Frank Shuman built a massive solar-powered plant which pumped 6,000 gallons of river water per minute onto cotton fields above the Nile. After Shuman's great success in Egypt, many thought solar energy was poised to make a big transition into popular usage (5).

Just before the outset of World War I in February of 1914, Shuman wrote in *Scientific American*: "Sun power is now a fact and no longer in the 'beautiful possibility' stage… (It will have) a history something like aerial navigation. The Wrights made an 'actual record' flight and thereafter developments were more rapid. We have made an 'actual record' in sun power and we also hope now for quick developments" (6).

Shuman's invention and his optimism were impressive and real, and solar power was poised to be adopted worldwide. But those plans were washed away by the coming of World War I. Immediately a high-powered, dense and mobile form of energy was necessary, so oil took precedence over solar, and notably, over coal power as well. The current political climate on the Earth is again tumultuous enough to pull our attention from the simple, clean, bountiful gift of solar energy, but the environmental decline that we are witnessing is necessarily waking us up to the need for sustainable energy.

Solar energy is limitless, and in a few days the sun showers us with enough sunlight to supply all of the Earth's energy needs for an entire year. It is totally environmentally friendly; after the cost of construction and installation, solar customers essentially receive free energy for decades. It allows all countries to have their own sustainable, independent energy source, which promotes self-sufficiency and helps to balance the global wealth gradient. And unlike fossil fuels, solar power requires very little transportation and distribution. Because solar energy can be stored in batteries or heat-retaining rock and mineral solutions, the variability of sunny or cloudy days becomes less of an issue. Homes can also remain connected to the traditional energy grid if they need additional energy at night.

The imminent benefits of solar energy are so grand that they are difficult to absorb: no wars over energy, no digging or drilling for energy, no more air pollution from carbon dioxide, no more oil spills, and very soon, no more high prices to air condition our homes and fuel our cars. This grand vision won't happen immediately, but solar power, along with other renewables, is the way to get there.

There are two principal ways that solar power is generated: using photovoltaic (PV) panels, or through concentrated solar power (CSP) plants. PV panels convert sunlight directly into electricity. CSP plants position hundreds of mirrors to reflect the sun's heat to a central tower, and that heat is used to boil water which produces steam. The steam rotates turbines which ultimately generate the electricity. Incidentally, boiling water to turn turbines is also involved in the coal and nuclear energy production processes, yet those energy sources generate massive amounts of pollution, while solar power emits none.

According to the European Union, two billion people

worldwide are not connected to the electric power grid. They are ideal candidates for local solar energy collection, since extending the traditional power grid infrastructure can be prohibitively costly. Countless solar energy projects are springing up in the developing world, principally for water pumping and electric lighting (7). There are currently around 900 solar plants globally which produce more than 200 kilowatts of energy, or enough to support 100 homes (8). The International Energy Agency predicts that solar power, which now provides only 0.5% of the world's electricity, will satisfy nearly one-fourth of global energy demand by 2050, according to a recent report.

In Japan, Germany, and the American Southwest, photovoltaic (PV) electricity is already utilized by over a million denizens, including a half million households in Germany alone. 150 schools in Germany now use photovoltaic systems for their energy needs as well (9). The US Coast Guard has 10,525 "stand-alone" PV systems, each saving taxpayers an estimated $5,000 over its lifetime, while Zaire's twenty-building Bulape Hospital is the world's first medical complex that is 100% solar powered (10). Near Barstow, California, there is a 300-foot tower encircled by almost 2000 giant mirrors, called heliostats, comprising a concentrated solar power (CSP) plant. This plant generates ten megawatts (MW) of electricity, which is enough to light 3,000 homes in Southern California. Other CSP projects include the Desertec Coalition's 250 million Euro, 150 megawatt facility 100 miles south of Cairo, Egypt, and a 400 megawatt plant by Bright Source Energy that will power 140,000 homes in California (11). Bright Source has already signed a contract with Southern California Edison to provide $800 million worth of electricity per year to the Los Angeles area. At 50 megawatts, the largest photovoltaic plant on the planet is Almedilla de Alarcon in Spain (12). While, as early as 1991, photovoltaic systems were used by thirty-five U.S. utility companies (13).

Renewable energy in general, including wind, biomass, geothermal, wave, and solar power, is growing very rapidly. Iceland's use of geothermal and hydroelectric energy is advancing to the point that they are flirting with being the globe's first society that is free of fossil fuels entirely. According to the U.S. Department of Energy, wind and solar power production in the U.S. are both growing over ten times faster than traditional energy production from fossil fuels. Globally, wind and solar power are growing at approximately 20-30% per year (14). Denmark and Germany lead the world in wind production, with Denmark getting a full two-thirds of its energy from wind (15). Worldwide investments in so-called "clean tech," or renewable energies, leaped from $28.3 billion in 2004 to $94.5 billion by 2007 (16). By the year 2030, some estimates suggest that renewables could supply up to fifty percent of America's energy needs (17). President Obama is determined to make that shift a reality within his tenure, which is very encouraging.

Biomass energy generation -- essentially the production of ethanol and biodiesel fuels -- is also a significant source of energy, and accounts for up to half of renewable energy production in some regions of the world. Corn or sugar is usually the raw material for ethanol, and biodiesel is most commonly made from soybean oil or algae. One limitation is that most forms of biomass energy production remove nutrients from the soil and compete with food for cropland, which may inhibit their implementation long term. However, ethanol made from rice husks and other agricultural or forestry waste products does not have this drawback, nor does biodiesel made from algae. It is estimated that forestry waste alone could annually produce 18 billion gallons of ethanol (18). Also sustainably viable is biodiesel fuel made from used restaurant cooking oil, which is voluminous in Western nations.

In the words of visionary billionaire businessman, Ted Turner, "Our future depends on changing the way we use energy. We've got to move away from fossil fuels and develop long-term energy solutions that work. Using clean energy technologies such as solar power is the right thing to do, and it represents a tremendous business opportunity" (19).

One concept that I always convey to my students at Cal State University, Northridge is that renewable energies and fossil fuels are all simply sunlight stored in different forms. Fossil fuels are dead plants and animals which have decayed and condensed over millions of years into fossilized form. Plants survive by converting the sun's energy into chemical energy through photosynthesis, and animals survive by consuming this stored energy in plants. Therefore, the "life force" in plant and animal remains, or fossil fuels, is simply ancient, degraded, condensed sunlight. Hence, oil and coal are ancient sunlight stored in liquid or solid form. Solar energy is fresh, un-degraded and utilizable sunlight in its highest and purest energy form. The fact that using fresh solar energy generates essentially no negative effects on the environment, while burning decayed, old, fossilized solar energy (principally oil and coal) pollutes the air, damages living things, and is causing the globe to heat up are clear signs from nature guiding us to the best form of the sun's power.

In 2008, the total amount of energy consumed worldwide was 474 exajoules, which is equivalent to about ten billion metric tons of oil (20)(21). 37% of this energy comes from oil, 25% from coal, 23% from natural gas, 6% nuclear, and about 9% from the renewable sources of water, wind, and sunlight. The United States has only 5% of the world's population yet consumes 25% of its energy, making us the biggest energy consumers and wasters on the planet. It is generally estimated that world oil supply will be exhausted within a few to several decades, yet most sources predict that coal supplies will last up to two more centuries. Thus, the concept of clean renewable energy – energy derived from the sun and from the movement of wind and water – is so attractive. One example of more efficient living is metropolitan Tokyo's aggressive mandate that 1,400 Tokyo factories and office buildings cut their carbon emissions 25% by 2020. (22). The mandate's carbon cap-and-trade arrangement is the first implemented by any major metro area.

One solar provider in Southern California called "Pure Current" is creating a small revolution in the energy market by improving the efficiency of the electric grid, one home or business at a time. The company places a converter box on your home that synergizes the various incoming streams of electric current (from the grid or from your own solar panels) and reduces friction and waste by up to 25%. This adds up to huge savings for the home or business owner, as well as significant reductions in overall CO2 production.

Besides pollution produced from burning fossil fuels, the mere acquisition of these fuels also has myriad negatives. Author Jennifer Carless suggests that since national security is such an issue of late, energy self-sufficiency should be our first goal, because then need for foreign military invasion would profoundly diminish (23). Also, close to three trillion dollars have been spent on the Iraq war alone, which any analyst would agree is related to the acquisition of oil. Hence, the taxpayers ultimately foot the bill, as well as deal with the terrorist retaliation, of these ventures. Military action has played an important role in America's social and economic evolution and certainly in the assurance of many domestic liberties. Yet it is inappropriate and unnecessary for our military to be used to steal energy at gunpoint from the Middle East, especially when solar energy is raining down for free every day all across our fifty states.

In "The Greenhouse Effect" published by Greenpeace, they state that if we continue with current levels of fossil fuel use and environmental degradation, "the world will be unlike anything in human history." They mention that massive climatic change along with changes in ocean temperatures and currents would cause rampant species extinctions worldwide. In the U.S. specifically, large areas of eastern and southern forests may be destroyed, and the Midwestern grain belt would become a desert (24). Consequently, according to eminent biologist E.O. Wilson, 50% of plant and animal species on Earth will be extinct by 2100.

Authors Martin Katzman and Travis Bradford describe this slew of negative effects from using fossil fuels as "social costs" and "loaded costs," respectively (25). They include that these costs to society and the environment must be taken into account by those who decide on energy policy, and by the general public who ultimately decide which energy source to use. In his book, *Solar Revolution*, Bradford specifically cites the grave ramifications, such as terrorism, of acquiring traditional energy supplies through military action (26).

Many oil advocates emphasize that the initial cost of conversion to solar energy will be impractical and expensive. Yet these advocates should notice that the globe is already converting, but in another way – we are converting to a world with alarming levels of pollution, rising sea levels, perennial wars over energy, as well as skyrocketing asthma cases from pollution and skin cancer levels from ozone depletion.

For purely economic reasons, many predict that the world's transition to solar energy will be precipitously fast. "Increasingly and dramatically over the next few decades... consumers will turn directly to the sun for their energy. This will happen not because solar power is clean and green but because basic economic and political reasons compel us to make this choice. At the point that the out-of-pocket real cash cost of solar electricity drops below the costs of current conventional energy alternatives (a situation that is already occurring in the Japanese residential electricity market), the adoption speed of solar energy will rival nearly every technological leap in history" (27). Thin-film solar technology is one example of an advancement that is dramatically dropping the price of producing solar apparatus. The process is based on applying an alloy called CIGS (for copper-indium-gallium-selenide) in an extremely thin layer on flexible surfaces. Industry experts say that CIGS could revolutionize our energy production policies within just a few years.

Being a major source of resistance to the solar age, oil company fears could be assuaged by the prospect of shifting their ingenuity and capitalist desires to the development of the most efficient and marketable photovoltaic cells. Shell Oil seems to agree with the promise of renewable energy's future in that they periodically invest large sums in solar and wind production. Chevron and British Petroleum are following suit. Defense contractors such as Ceradyne, in lieu of supplying the military with industrial ceramics to be used as armor, has plans to manufacture solar-receiving apparatus when wartime ends (28).

War, global instability, and avarice of those who control energy and resources have delayed the world's conversion to solar energy for many decades. Frank Shuman's progress with solar power in the early 1900s was stymied by the chaos and instability of the First World War. Today is little different. We are perennially posited in a state of war and fear of war. This generates feelings of protection, territorialism, and divisiveness: an environment which favors the providers of existing and familiar channels of energy. In 19th century Europe, despite supply limitations, plant strikes, and other problems with coal, European rulers and governments did not seek out alternative sources of energy but instead "hunkered down" and did their best to control and monopolize all that was left of this dwindling resource (29).

This is precisely what is happening with oil in the 20th century. A litany of oil-related environmental problems are demonstrating that the end of the oil age is arriving. Rather than acknowledging the ubiquity, environmental affinity, and low cost of solar energy, the oil giants are helping to promote

gas-guzzling vehicles, actively suppressing media coverage
of virtually constant oil leaks and spills, and squeezing
every last penny out of their brief and lucrative monopoly. I
commend these companies for their intermittent investment
in renewables, but much more is called for. It is difficult to
peer through the fog created by so much distraction, conflict,
and escalated demand surrounding oil, but it is the prerogative
of individuals and leaders, especially in the powerful and
resource-consumptive West, to see through this haze. The time
has come to consciously and definitively take global energy in
a new, benevolent, and renewable direction. The clear standout
among the cohort of sustainable energy options is solar power.

The Second Way to Save the Planet

Eat Organic: It heals our bodies and our soils. Organic food does not contain the pesticides and herbicides that contribute to the high cancer rates of industrialized countries, nor does it contain the high fructose corn syrup or trans-fatty acids that are leading to obesity and diabetes. The prevalence of these diseases is overwhelming our health care system. A significant increase in consumption of organic food would save billions of dollars in reduced health care costs every year. Moreover, going organic heals our soils all over the planet that have been depleted and polluted by over-farming and excessive chemicals for decades. Organic farming's crop rotation and fallow period along with the absence of polluting chemicals restores health and productivity to the soil exactly when we need it most – to feed our planet's exploding population. Sustainability is the key because soil is essentially a non-renewable resource.

Organic Agriculture

"The Lord God took the man and put him in the Garden of Eden to till it and keep it."

- Genesis 2:15

I had never seen food this beautiful before. Cherries, pears, arugula, mushrooms, and a lush abundance of other fruits and vegetables adorned the racks as I stood in the back cooler at *Chez Panisse* in Berkeley, California -- one of America's first all-organic, gourmet restaurants. I had earned a one-day tryout in which I would prepare the morel mushroom pasta sauce for the vegetarian menu option that evening at this famous prix-fixe establishment. The care and skill that the team of renowned chefs displayed when discussing and preparing food was both impressive and endearing to me. But even more impressive was the crate after crate of vibrant, fresh, organic produce that was being delivered throughout the day. The restaurant's trend-setting fame is a testament to the foresight of its owner and vehement "locavore," Alice Waters.

My tryout was a success, but I ended up finding a better permanent fit as manager of a nearby raw and organic café called *Raw Energy*. It always struck me how physically different my clientele at *Raw Energy* looked compared to the customers at, say, a fast food restaurant, or even a mainstream grocery store. If the skin, eyes, and energy level of my clients were any testament, there is definitely something different, and better for us, about eating organic food. *Chez Panisse* and *Raw Energy* are still in existence and thriving, and my experience at both locations fortified my love of healthy organic food which has only increased in the decade following.

Throughout history before the twentieth century, all of the farms on Earth were organic. And until the last fifty years, the vast majority of people on Earth were, in fact, farmers. Domesticated agriculture began about 10,000 years ago but has experienced massive changes in this most recent century due to the astronomical rise in global population. Yields have had to increase, so mechanization and chemicals became integral to many wealthy nations' food cultivation practices. This approach, culminating in a sense with the Green Revolution of the 80s and 90s, proved very successful at increasing yields. Yet in its wake, with a few decades of perspective, the negative effects of this industrial-scale conventional agriculture are now observable – namely, pesticide-contaminated soils, water supplies and food, as well as topsoil loss on a grand scale, and a population that has consumed harmful chemical-laden food for years.

Due to these proven deleterious effects on the environment and on the health of the general human population, a return to agriculture that is in harmony with nature began. Organic agriculture, also called sustainable agriculture, is that natural method. Employed most pervasively and extensively in Europe, organic agriculture is attractive essentially for its positive health benefits and for its beneficial effect and symbiotic relationship with the environment. It has become a $30 billion industry world-wide, and is growing at 15-30% annually (1).

Organic farming has a few essential characteristics. Very simply, organic farmers do *not* use chemical fertilizers, chemical pesticides, chemical herbicides, or genetically modified or engineered seeds. Four of the most important components that organic farmers *do* utilize are the following: growing a wide variety of crops, rotating crops, using only natural fertilizers (manure or compost), and being vertically integrated wherein ownership, labor, packaging, and distribution often co-exist all on one site (2). Rotating crops allows soil to replenish itself naturally, as different crops pull different nutrients from the soil each growing season. Rotation aids in natural pest and weed control, as well. Also, like all pre-20th century farms, organic farms always leave a section of the land in fallow, or rest, so that it may fully recover before being planted again. This process helps humus, or decayed living matter, to develop in the soil, keeping soil moist and fertile. Without fallow or crop rotation, conventional farms need artificial fertilizers to keep depleted soils productive and chemical pesticides to kill resident bugs. Organic farms are also usually much smaller than conventional farms.

Most widely practiced in Europe, sustainable agriculture is also showing substantial growth in the developing world, with ninety developing countries now producing organic foods on a commercial scale. This trend is fueled both by an increasing demand in the first world for organic tropical foods and by an immediate need to curtail the damage to soils and water supplies wrought by decades of intensive conventional farming in equatorial nations. Some support for this organic movement has come from national governments, but the lion's share has come from benevolent non-governmental organizations and regional affiliations which are committed to this movement. The lure of big profits from large-scale chemical, or conventional, farming in the United States is gradually losing ground to the health benefits and environmental sustainability of the organic approach. Though it is growing significantly each year, organic production still only accounts for about one percent of total agricultural output in the U.S. (3).

Conventional farms are defined by huge acreages of mono-crops, heavy chemical additives such as synthetic fertilizers, pesticides and herbicides, and significant portions of yields coming from genetically modified or engineered seeds. Some positives of conventional farming are that its high mechanization frees up a large portion of the population for other endeavors, and it produces massive yields and surpluses which have helped to feed starving populations. Yet its negative effects cannot be ignored. Economically, small and medium-sized farms are disappearing as are rural communities, both of which exacerbate the already rapid rural-to-urban migration seen in the developing world. Also, farms are over-subsidized by the government. This means that surpluses are produced and crop prices fall, necessitating larger yields and hence larger amounts of chemical additives to the soil the following year. Environmentally, synthetic fertilizers kill living biota such as beneficial bacteria which are the life force of the soil, while pesticides and herbicides reside on food and filter into groundwater and streams. Moreover, chemical fertilizers and massive amounts of unutilized manure (from non-organic cattle feed lots) filter into waterways and then to the ocean where they metabolize all available oxygen and create giant "dead zones" for aquatic life.

Conventional farming, now termed "agri-business," has become inextricably and overwhelmingly motivated by money. In his book, *The Unsettling of America: Culture and Agriculture*, author Wendell Berry comments that "the economy of money has infiltrated and subverted the economies of nature, energy, and the human spirit" (4). Policy decisions seem to be made with complete disregard for the environment and only focused on larger yields and higher profits.

In 1979, the World Food Programme came about in order to find solutions to global hunger. Increasing the amount of food produced per acre of land was seen as the necessary end, and genetic modification of seeds was seen as the means to get there. In locations such as the International Rice Research Institute in the Philippines, huge amounts of financing went into the development of genetically modified organisms, or GMOs. GMOs are seeds that are genetically altered by splicing in DNA from other plants and even animals in order to give the seeds certain traits, such as resistance to specific pests or more resilience during drought or frost. For instance, genes from a salmon may be inserted into a corn plant, or genes from a sweet potato may be spliced into a fruit tree. These seeds allow for higher yields and less need for adherence to nature's indices and cycles, yet it is unknown what effect these gene-spliced organisms are having on human beings.

In the words of author Leslie Duram,

"With no long-term safety studies, we've introduced these new genetically-altered materials to our environment and into our bodies. We simply do not have the facts on GMOs, yet we are currently conducting a massive experiment on you, me, the rest of society, and our ecosystems. Organic agriculture and buying organic food are the only way to avoid being part of this global experiment...(which is) being driven by the profit motives of several agribusiness and pharmaceutical corporations"(5).

In organic agriculture, naturally, GMO crops are never cultivated. A large proportion of nations across the globe will not accept GMO crops because they are wary of the possible negative effects and leery of the lack of long-term testing on these relatively new plants. In the United States, however, GMO crops abound with 72% of all GMO crops on Earth being grown in this country. In fact, 40% of corn, 73% of cotton, and over 90% of soybeans in the U.S. are GMO crops (6). Genetically modified organisms are not labeled in the U.S. because, curiously, the USDA does not require it, nor has the USDA done any long-term research on the effects of GMOs on people or the environment.

Many of these biotech firms are substantial contributors to political campaigns, and the principal way that they make money is to "patent nature." That is, these companies are allowed to artificially generate a biological product, patent it, and thereby have exclusive rights to sell it. One cannot patent apples or corn as they occur in nature, so laboratory-produced versions of them are generated, advertised as superior, patented, and then sold. Biotech firms even spend millions on advertising which puts a positive "emotional" spin on genetically engineered foods (7).

What's more, farmers are forced to sign contracts with major GMO corporations, such as Monsanto, that state they will only use their brand of pesticides and that they will not use the seeds bought one year on the next year's crop. Some farmers are even sued because they are caught growing GMO crops without a contract. This industry has gone so far as to produce "suicidal genes," which cause a seed to self-destruct after several months, ensuring that it can only be used for a given year's planting (8). Although Monsanto is the largest producer of genetically engineered seeds, it began as a chemical company producing DDT and Agent Orange during the Vietnam War era. The company's genetic engineering of seeds began so they could modify and sell a soybean that was tolerant of its most profitable herbicide, called "Roundup." In 1996, two percent of U.S. soybeans contained the Monsanto "Roundup-ready" gene, but by 2008, over ninety percent of all soybeans in the U.S. contained the gene (9).

One significant positive result of the GMO movement is that it has increased yields on innumerable farms around the world. Many GMO scientists have earnestly magnanimous intentions that their food-engineering feats will feed the planet. Their efforts have, indeed, staved off starvation for perhaps millions of people for several years. That is a victory by any account. Yet this victory is necessarily short-lived, as the heavy chemicals applied to fields in order to produce these yields have so polluted and depleted soils as often to render them essentially infertile. Further marring the GMO victory party is that its seeds and chemical inputs are very expensive, so the process instantly puts farmers into a debt-dependency to biotech companies. There is a growing consensus that genetic engineering is simply another way for huge corporations to reap profits at the expense of the environment and the less fortunate. Evidence of impending monopoly is that over 70% of all GMO plants on the market today are designed to be tolerant of Monsanto's "Roundup" pesticide (10).

Dr. Tewolde, general manager of Ethiopia's Environmental Protection Authority, wrote that "GE (genetic engineering) threatens to make the problem (food insecurity) worse, creating dependence on corporate-owned agricultural inputs such as seed, decreasing the need for labor, decreasing agricultural diversity, promoting agribusiness over family farms... (etc)" (11).

In the United States as well as other industrialized nations such as Argentina, conventional farms receive billions of dollars in government subsidies (paid by taxpayers), and these subsidies are contingent upon the continuation of conventional farming techniques, often including the purchase of GMOs. Organic farming in the United States is not a recipient of such governmental aid.

In early 20th century Europe, like today, organic agriculture struggled to survive against the powerful chemical companies. This conflict was expressed most vividly when the "bio-dynamic" agricultural movement was banned by the Nazis beginning in 1940 due to pressure exerted upon them by the German chemical companies (12). The German government of that era was focused on generating the largest agricultural output possible in order to sustain economic and political prosperity, with the environment being essentially ignored (13). Soon, observations of the deleterious effects of such agriculture were commonplace, which coupled with an expanded demand for healthier foods to spur a resurgence of natural food cultivation in Europe. A similar conversion is happening now in the United States, despite heavy and continued legislative support of chemical agribusiness techniques.

As a geography professor, I find an organic farm to be the perfect environment in which to teach students how humans and the Earth work together in symbiosis. I bring about 100 of my students to Tierra Miguel organic farm each semester to plant, harvest, and taste everything from butter lettuce and carrots to cherry tomatoes and strawberries. About thirty minutes removed from the main highway in the Pauma Valley of southern California, the only sounds audible on the farm are the rustling of horses at a nearby stable, the occasional cry of a red-tailed hawk, and the wind itself. The knowing, healing timbres in the voices of the farm's owners, Mil and Leia Krecu, alone are worth the trip. A few students initially balk at the physical labor or the "dirt everywhere," but by the end of the day, I always witness a transformation, and many don't want to leave. Every vegetable grown on the farm is crisp and light. Every piece of fruit is juicy and sweet. And according to my students, once someone tastes food like this, they'll be hooked for life. Experience leads me to agree.

The proliferation of organic farms such as Tierra Miguel is actually even more widespread in Europe than in the U.S. In Switzerland, 11% of farms are organic. In Austria the number is 9% and in Denmark it is 6% (14). By comparison, less than 1% of U.S. farms are organic. Many public institutions like schools and hospitals in Europe are encouraged or required to purchase organic food (15).The demand for organic foods in Europe, especially in their cold winters, is so great that they have secured many developing world and otherwise warm climate sources for organic fruits and vegetables.

Beyond profiting from European demand, many nations in the developing world with large populations are turning to sustainable organic farming out of necessity. The high yields of conventional farming were a quick fix but now are proving quite unrealistic in the long run. In China's Changjiang Valley, 2.4 billion tons of topsoil have been lost to surface runoff, prompting the United Nations Environment Program to intervene and implement an eco-farming agenda (16). Shifting cultivation, terracing, and crop rotation and diversification are now utilized. Sustainable farming is an easy fit for the developing world, in that it matches well with the natural, centuries-old farming practices that have existed for millennia in much of the tropics. The knowledge, skill base, and ample labor force necessary to implement organic farming on a large scale are all present in the world's developing nations.

Over the past two decades, Cuba is a very impressive example of an underdeveloped nation wholeheartedly and successfully adopting organic agriculture. Since Soviet-subsidized conventional production proved environmentally unsound and unable to feed its population, Cuba has enlisted its sizeable scientific community to conduct extensive research on organic farming methods. Hundreds of regional facilities now produce bio-pesticides, which are natural bacterial and fungal diseases that kill insects. Cuba is the only country in the hemisphere, as of the mid 1990s, to use microbial antagonists on a large scale to counter soil-borne plant disease (17). Organic fertilizers, composting of garbage from cities, and humus production by earthworm composts are further evidence of Cuba's all-inclusive dedication to this agricultural modality. It is a convincing display of how rapidly a nation can transition from conventional to organic farming when the government and industry join forces. In the case of Cuba, a communist country, government and industry are essentially one in the same. Cuban officials estimate that with this kind of unilateral decision, any nation can convert to 100% organic in three to five years.

The Cuban government offers financial incentives to

urbanites who agree to move to the countryside to provide the increased labor necessary for organic agriculture. The augmented need for rural labor has huge implications for stemming the massive rural-to-urban migration in the developing world today.

I personally began eating organic food about ten years ago, and my diet has varied from 20% - 80% organic over the years. I have noticed several changes in my body, some significant and some subtle. First, I am undeniably leaner. Chemicals on food which are unidentifiable to the body are often stored in fatty tissues. When I cleansed my body by simply ingesting fewer and fewer chemicals, I also shed some fat in the process. In addition, I noticed that eating organic fruits and vegetables gave my skin better protection from the sun and improved the appearance of my skin in general. In fact, about three months after I began drinking fresh organic juices, people began to comment that my skin looked healthier. Overall, my physical endurance increased, my system just felt cleaner, and I seemed to wake up feeling more refreshed as a result of eating more organic food.

For the consumer who is wondering, "Where can I buy organic food near me?" the answer is at your local farmer's market, Trader Joe's or Whole Foods markets. You can also become part of a CSA (Community Supported Agriculture) in which you pay a local organic farm around $20 every two weeks to deliver to you a large box full of whatever has been freshly picked on the farm.

Countless studies have proven the nutritional superiority of eating organic. In a study that investigated forty-one previous nutritional studies published in the *Journal of Alternative and Complimentary Medicine,* organic crops were shown to contain substantially more vitamin C, iron, magnesium, phosphorous, and usable protein than conventional crops (18). Specific organic crops such as strawberries, blackberries, and corn have been shown to contain more antioxidants than their conventional counterparts (19). In addition, a study done in the U.S. divulged that people who have eaten an organic diet excrete flavinoids and show signs of antioxidant activity. That is, they have more antioxidants in their system (20).

One pro-organic author, in commenting on depleted conventionally-produced foods, states, "Given that most Americans eat conventionally-produced food, the diminished vitamin and mineral content of this food could lead to long-term nutritional inferiority and adverse health effects" (21). Also, organic livestock do not get antibiotics in huge doses like conventionally-raised animals, so they don't contribute to the development of resistant microorganisms. Even without antibiotic-infused animals and chemical pest control on crops, there is no increased risk of food poisoning in organic food (22). Organic crops also show lower levels of nitrates and heavy metals (23).

The quantifiable superiority of organic foods often has scientific explanation, such as pesticide presence shutting down the production of certain antioxidants, like phenols, in plants. Chemicals also kill biota and diminish humus, which are the living components of the soil. Yet it seems clear that there are other intangible elements at play. For example, in a commonly replicated test, people who eat home-made chicken soup as opposed to canned chicken soup recover faster from the influenza virus, a.k.a. the common cold. Is it the human care and love that goes into the home-cooked meal that speeds recovery? I became aware of a very similar effect with organic food when I managed Raw Energy organic café and came to know several of my organic farmer suppliers. I would hear them talking about their farm or soil as if it were a loved one:

"Yeah, she's beautiful. I've been spending a lot of time with her lately and she's recovered well. She's ready. I mean, just look at these cabbages!"

The food from those farmers almost seemed to glow with their love. I felt good about serving it to my customers. Could that love possibly be the cause of the higher antioxidant counts and more vitamins and minerals in organic foods? It's difficult to prove scientifically, but in my opinion, it is absolutely possible.

One last point is that organic farms are often critiqued to be not as profitable as conventional ones. However, organic farms do not receive the massive financial support from the federal government that conventional farms enjoy, so reversing this subsidy advantage would make organic sites vastly more profitable. With this uneven playing field, organic farms are sometimes less profitable in the short term, yet frequently more profitable in the medium and long term than conventional farm companies. In a study done in France in 2000, it was found that organic farms were often just as profitable as conventional ones, especially in the long run (24). Moreover, the organic farming process actually improves the soil, whereas soils that have been farmed conventionally for decades are commonly severely depleted (especially in the U.S. South). Therefore, when the notion of profitability goes beyond just money and includes the natural resources of an area and the health of its residents, organic farming is far and away the more viable option (25).

In conclusion, it is becoming apparent that an expanded focus on organic, sustainable cultivation is now an inevitable future for global agriculture. An encouraging sign was that by the year 2000, more organic food was sold in mainstream supermarkets than in natural-food stores, marking its shift into mainstream consumption. Also, thanks to the efforts of First Lady, Michelle Obama, the White House front lawn now contains an organic garden. As farmers and food shoppers increasingly acquiesce to the overwhelming environmental, economic, and social benefits of organic foods, a profound shift is occurring in the way that we grow and consume food on this planet. Hopefully this transition will not be one of begrudged economic necessity, but rather one of conscientious and preemptive decision making on the part of industry and government leaders as well as consumers who have the power to fully manifest such a change.

The Third Way to Save the Planet

Give: Donate money or time to non-governmental organizations (NGOs) that focus on helping the developing world. This bridges the global gap between rich and poor by allowing resources to flow from the "haves" to the "have-nots." It is the best way to directly help the one-fourth of the world that is starving, without basic human rights, and dying by the thousands every day. Your giving also helps impoverished countries to develop economically by becoming more self-sufficient and sustainably productive. With better options for income in these nations, the lure of deforestation, animal poaching, or entering the drug or sex trades will diminish. These harmful choices are simply examples of desperately poor people trying to survive. NGOs are critical because they take action, even when it is deemed politically unsavory or economically imprudent for national governments to do so. Moreover, several NGOs help to prosecute human rights abuses and war crimes, both of which show humanity's darkest side.

Benevolent Individuals
The Oprah Winfrey Factor

Didier Drogba, a striker for England's Chelsea Football Club, has pledged to donate all of his endorsement earnings to build hospitals in his native Cote d'Ivoire. Malalai Joya is a woman who defied the Taliban by earning a seat in Afghanistan's Parliament and starting underground schools to educate girls, while Michael Pritchard is a Brit who invented the "Lifesaver Bottle" which can provide millions of people in the developing world with inexpensive, lifesaving, clean water (1).

Powerful, progressive, and magnanimous individuals are a critical part of the equation for the continuing evolution of this planet. Any individual has the power to uplift others. Some uplift a friend or spouse. Some uplift a classroom or a household. The will of a good quarterback can inspire a team to a victory, while the powerful spirit of a good preacher can lift a whole community. Individuals are needed and called upon at all levels of leadership and inspiration. Presidents and other national-scale leaders have innumerable times changed the course of their people's vision, focus, morale, or even their history. And there have been a few individuals who exhibited the power to uplift the entire world. We all know their names.

The power of individuals to uplift is mighty, and one way that they do this is through giving money – whether they are billionaires or bellboys. The Guggenheims, John D.

Rockefeller III, and Andrew Carnegie financially supported everything from aviation and space rocketry to penicillin and guaranteed pensions for teachers. Victor Pinchuk, Ukranian millionaire, personally funded his nation's first grand-scale contemporary art center, its first private chamber orchestra, as well as a nationally televised concert, together with Elton John, to promote AIDS awareness. On the other side of the giving coin is the March of Dimes which was funded by the pocket change of literally millions of donors and resulted in the first polio vaccine (2). In addition, half of all hospital beds, 95% of all orchestras, and 60% of all social service organizations are funded by private individuals (3).

The United States has the most generous citizens in the world, in that they donate a much larger percentage of their GDP than the denizens of any other country. 89% of Americans made donations in 2001, totaling $177 billion (4). By 2003, that number had risen to $240 billion, according to Forbes. com. Author Claire Gaudiani suggests that Americans are not generous because they are rich -- rather, that they are rich because they are generous (5). That is, philanthropy throughout the generations in this country has largely been directed beyond immediate aid and toward investing in our human and infrastructural capital. For instance, private donations sent many prominent Americans to college, such as Ralph Waldo Emerson, Alice Walker, Oprah Winfrey, Itzhak Perlman, and Bill Clinton. These people all went on to considerably enrich the lives of both Americans and citizens of the globe.

Many leaders and persons who uplift do so through action and not just through monetary donation. Often a tragedy or tragic era provides the opportunity for a true leader or hero to rise up. The Nazi reign in Europe and the era of slavery in the U.S. produced heroes such as Arthur Schindler and Elie Weisel, and Harriet Tubman and Frederick Douglass, respectively. In fact, noting the geographic source of historical "heroes" leads us to the most poignant sites of suffering.

Mohandes Ghandi, Nelson Mandela, and Stephen Biko all originally fought for minority rights in South Africa, a hyper-segregated and highly discriminative country at the time. Martin Luther King, Jr., Malcolm X, and Rosa Parks pushed for the civil rights of American Blacks in the separate but still unequal United States of the 1960s.

Today we see prominent figures such as Oprah Winfrey, Al Gore, Michael Moore, and Glenn Beck who are changing the way we think and countering many widely accepted beliefs. What does their prominence say about the current social climate in this country? What are they fighting against? Michael Moore is very controversial because he pushes hard for governmental and public policy transparency. Both Moore and Glenn Beck, though politically polar opposites, are powerful forces which are galvanizing the public to take part in, or even just take notice of, the management of its country. That Moore's documentaries are viewed on such a mass scale is a testament to how shrouded and clandestine the operations of our government have been.

Some altruists are fighting – and winning -- battles that most of us are not even aware of. Aung San Suu Kyi has tirelessly defended democracy within dictatorial Myanmar for the majority of her life. While separated from her family under house arrest in Myanmar for over fourteen years, she managed to be elected prime minister and be awarded the 1991 Nobel Peace Prize. In India, Dr. Perumalsamy Namperumalsamy's patient list is even longer than his name. His eye-care hospitals have performed 3.6 million cataracts surgeries, giving sight to the previously blind (6). While South Africa's Elon Musk is both a NASA rocket scientist and a green pioneer. He designed the all-electric Tesla sports car and helped to create Solar City, the largest residential provider of solar power in the U.S

Specific events can also elicit and necessitate new ways of helping and interacting with each other. The Hurricane Katrina and September 11 tragedies are such examples here in the U.S. These disasters were so large in scale that no individual, organization, or government could handle the care, reparations and recovery alone. We necessarily had to *collaborate* in order to significantly help. Organizations public and private, profit and non-profit, governmental and individual, all came together to begin to repair our torn cities of New York and New Orleans. This showed us a precedent for how we must handle our nation and our world in the future…together. This topic is elucidated by *Collaborative Philanthropies* author Elwood Hopkins.

The confluence of different players to bring a larger goal to reality is becoming more common in corporate America. The pith of this trend is seen clearly in the television show *Extreme Makeover, Home Edition*. Behind the façade of a home-makeover show, this giant production finds families with specific and deep needs and builds fully-amenitied homes for them in a single week. This alone is an encouraging sight, but even more inspiring is that most of the necessary labor, appliances, and building materials are donated to the show. This, of course, is often coupled with advertising space on the show, which is naturally good for business. And that's the amazing part of it – there is now a precedent that being benevolent is good for business! That is a revolutionary, palpable, immediate, and emotional realization, and it is masterfully presented to us by the ABC *Extreme Makeover* production team. Corporate philanthropy certainly has a tradition of benefiting a company's image, but never so immediately and effectively as through this particular medium and method. Examples like *Extreme Makeover* as well as a recent collaboration between Target, the Salvation Army, and magician David Blaine are blazing a trail for future altruistic efforts. These projects set an important precedent showing that collaborative philanthropies can generate a cascade of varied and positive effects and, simply, that giving is beneficial for everyone involved.

In many aspects of the recovery effort after Katrina and 9/11, individuals took the lead if and when the government showed a lethargic response. This exhibits the power and the vector of the benevolent individual in our world today. Many governments are still engrossed in the lure of territorial and financial conquest through military action and economic subjugation. The United States has the positive effect of spreading ideas of equal rights and democracy, yet it has also spent nearly three trillion dollars and almost ten years warring with two small countries in central Asia. So while many prominent governments are otherwise occupied, powerful and magnanimous individuals have stepped up and taken it upon themselves to incite change.

Countless families and individuals throughout this country's and this globe's history have had a profound benevolent impact, from the Medecis of Renaissance Italy to the Guggenheims, McLeods, Fords, Rockefellers, Packards, Carnegies, and Kelloggs of 20th century America. Noteworthy donors in the 21st century are Gordon and Betty Moore who have given $7 billion to environmental conservation, Michael and Susan Dell who gave $1 billion to children's health and education, and Alfred Mann, who has given over $800 million for biomedical research.

Even if you are a family of four earning $50,000 a year, you are a wealthy potential benefactor from the perspective of the world's one billion people living in abject poverty. In the Los Angeles area, my students at California State University, Northridge and my sister Stephanie's students at El Camino College, each gave one dollar this semester to our small organization called "Student Giving Tree." The organization operates through Kiva.org, a website that connects developing world residents in need of microloans with first world donors. In total, we sent around $350 this semester to six microloan recipients in Tanzania, Nicaragua, Peru, Cambodia, Bolivia, and Kenya. Those monetary amounts may not sound sizeable to most of us, but they can make a world of difference.

A few outstanding individuals today clearly have the intention and the ability to change the world: Ted Turner, Bill Gates, Al Gore, Greg Mortenson, and Oprah Winfrey. The philanthropy of Ted Turner in this century is, in short, amazing. He is magnanimous, outspoken, always quick to smile, and he walks and talks with the same swagger as John Wayne in an old Western. Turner amassed his fortune in the cable television and news industry. The innovator of twenty-four hour news, he saw his network's information delivery as a public service and he saw movies and cartoons (Turner classics on his TNT station) as able to carry TV viewers to "magical places" (7).

Christine Amanpour, who joined Turner's news station, CNN, in 1983, said "The idea of 24-hour news and global news is his creation. That's changed the world. It's changed people's relations with their governments. It's meant that governments can no longer crack down with impunity on protests" (8). Yet his service to society goes much further than magical movies and news channels. Turner has a deep desire both to protect the environment and to halt and reverse nuclear proliferation. His commitment to global peace is so great that in 1997, Ted Turner walked into United Nation's Secretary Kofi Anan's office and said "I'm going to give you a billion dollars," which he proceeded to do, with a $100 million donation each year for ten years (9).

He is also a tireless defender of and donor to environmental issues. In 2001 alone, the Turner Foundation gave almost $70 million to environmental causes (10). More recently, Turner joined with an Atlanta-based company to form "Southern Turner Renewable Energy," which will complete a thirty megawatt photovoltaic solar plant in New Mexico in late 2010. The plant will provide emission-free energy to 9,000 homes in the area (11). This portrait of magnanimity has also helped to spur other large-scale donations. Turner publicly urged other American billionaires to "loosen up their wads" which helped to jolt Bill Gates into a philanthropic state. Eventually Gates donated $25 billion, principally toward world health and the population explosion.

Al Gore is known for being the former Vice President and was very nearly put into office as the President of the United States. Yet at his core, he is a defender of the environment and he has utilized his political celebrity to further that mission. He cares for the soil, the water, the air, and the living inhabitants of the Earth as if it were his personal responsibility to do so. His best-selling book, "Earth in the Balance," was a wake-up call to many two decades ago, and it divulged his commitment to all things natural. Beyond just a galvanizing movie, Gore's documentary, "An Inconvenient Truth," is a strong admonishment to those who play a part in the trashing of our global environment and a universal call to duty for all to help heal it.

Neither a political figure nor a billionaire, Greg Mortenson, author of *Three Cups of Tea*, is nonetheless making the world a better place. Greg was saved by the kindness of a small Pakistani village who nurtured him back to health after he almost died while climbing K2 in 1993. Since then, he has devoted his life to building and funding schools, 131 of them to date, in Pakistan and Afghanistan. He has been awarded Pakistan's highest civil award, the Star of Pakistan, and has twice been nominated for the Nobel Peace Prize.

The changes that these visionary leaders bring about allow us to see that ideas and visions stimulate the confluence of people to fulfill a larger goal and new realities. Stanford University economist, Paul Romer, proposed the idea that an economy is founded on ideas rather than on tangible things (12). Those with good ideas are looking for the money to actualize their visions, while the wealthy are searching for deserving, ambitious individuals whom they can support. This union is what makes philanthropy so essential to the progress of a society. As mentioned before, Oprah Winfrey went to college on the donation of a private individual, and now her ideas and presence uplift millions or even billions of people. It is quite interesting and also beneficial to a society when a member of the downtrodden rises to the level of "royalty." This is indeed part of the plan for the healing and re-balancing of the world today. The meek shall inherit the Earth.

Certainly if anyone has gone from meager beginnings to fame, wealth, and altruism, it is Oprah. She began as a poor African-American girl from the segregated South and went on to become, in the words of CNN and Time.com "arguably the world's most powerful woman." In this author's opinion, Oprah Winfrey is this country's greatest philanthropist in the true sense of the word – a lover of man. *Business Week* named her the greatest black philanthropist in U.S. history, and *Time* magazine cited her as one of only four people who have shaped both the 20th and 21st centuries. But what Oprah gives to the world goes beyond money or celebrity or any specific cause – she is simply a powerful loving presence, and an example of how to live. She has fully developed her personal capital and she is a spiritually-connected, self-expressed and magnanimous individual. Amidst this era's barrages of negative news and propagation of fear of other countries, religions, and even of our next door neighbor, Oprah goes against that tide and encourages us to expect and highlight the good in each other and in the world.

To date, Oprah's Angel Network has raised over $51 million. In 2005 she gave away $250 million of her own money, $10 million of that to the Katrina relief effort (13). She has built a girls' school in South Africa and she spent $7 million putting 100 black men through college (14). The March 22, 2002 edition of *Christianity Today* called Ms. Winfrey "The Church of 'O,' a post-modern priestess – an icon of church-free spirituality." Very simply, it just feels good to wake up and know that Oprah is in the world, and that she's up to something good.

Besides just these individuals, entire groups of people have indeed risen up. Witness the plight of black Americans in general. Their labor provided the foundation for the building of this nation's industrialization and 19th century economic dominion, yet they suffered harsh discrimination and second-class citizen status for centuries. Today, the black culture is so pervasive in America and the world, due largely to its dissemination through music, movies, and television, that is has become indistinguishable from American culture itself. That is to say that in some ways, black culture is now at the helm of American popular culture. Moreover, black women's financial, societal, and spiritual rise in recent decades has been remarkable relative to their contemporary cohorts. Their particular rise has pulled this country up by its bootstraps by lifting black women, who author Zora Neale Hurston once called "the mule of the world," into a position of power, prominence, and leadership.

In today's United States, the Mexican and Central American population is present on all socio-economic levels, though principally represented in the working class. They are now the backs that break each day to provide the labor and services that this country needs to thrive. Besides the wealth of Latino history and culture that has already benefited this nation, what significant contributions will the Latino community bring to this country in the coming decades?

To conclude this idea of uplifting someone that they might uplift you in the future, a story about two young British boys may prove very encouraging. A wealthy family lived on a large 19th century English estate, and the estate grounds and home were tended to by a man, his wife and their children. The two families had sons of similar age and the boys would regularly play together. Despite not being able to swim, one day the wealthy boy jumped into the family pond, and immediately began to struggle to stay afloat. The other boy eventually saw this struggle and rushed in to save the young heir at the point of drowning. The parents were so thankful that they said to the servant father that they would fulfill any one request that he had, no matter how large. Having a strong belief in the importance of education, he immediately said, "Send my son to medical school."

The son of the estate-owning family eventually grew up to be Winston Churchill, and he led his entire nation to victory in World War II. One day during the early 1940s, in the thrust of the war, Winston drew ill. Quite fortuitously, penicillin had just been discovered by Alexander Fleming, a British doctor and medical researcher. Doctor Fleming himself was summoned to Mr. Churchill's side to administer the shot and assess his health. A few days later the doctor returned to find Winston up and about and healthy. At the wizened doctor's approach, Winston leaned close and whispered "That's the second time you've saved my life, Dr. Fleming."

We never know when our donation of love or money or support will be the springboard to another's greatness. Nor can we perhaps imagine what magnificence will be unleashed when we do so and how it will affect, or even save, our own life. So as individuals, communities, and nations, who can we raise up now that will in turn uplift us in the future? Who among us is so gifted that they will change the way we live and think, if only we give them the start they need? What hero is waiting for your gift, your attention, your love? Are you the next great benefactor, or are you the hero who waits to bloom? Either way, now is the time to share your gifts with the world.

Benevolent Organizations

"Our fight is not against any country, but a fight against hunger, suffering, desperation, and poverty."

- George C. Marshall, 1945, addressing Harvard University about the "Marshall Plan" for Europe's recovery from WWII.

An acquaintance of mine went to India in the 1980s in order to research family planning and population control strategies in rural communities. He came upon one farmer's humble abode, surrounded by a barely-standing fence on a remote dirt road in northern India. In his best Hindi, my friend greeted the man, described the regional benefits of birth control, and after conveying their utility, left him with about fifty condoms. Returning to the same house about a month later to check on the farmer's progress, my friend immediately saw that all of the condoms had been used, but not exactly as he had hoped. One condom had been carefully unrolled over each fencepost in the front of the house as a symbolic shield against the arrival of new children! The language barrier in this simple interaction had clearly proven to be a larger hurdle than anticipated.

This is an excellent example of how well-funded policies need adept, grassroots implementation in thousands of locations across the world in order to be successful. National governments provide large sums of international aid, to their credit, yet it is often unequally distributed, embezzled by local rulers, or spent on programs that simply don't synergize well with the local culture. Also, it can be difficult for governments to remove politics from aid, as many still toil in territorial conflict, economic competition, and a propagation of the "zero-sum game" mentality. As a result, many groups were born which went under, around, and beyond national governments in their efforts and implementations of helping to ameliorate some of the lack and injustice that was being witnessed in the world.

These groups are most commonly known as NGOs, or non-governmental organizations, but are perhaps more aptly described as benevolent international organizations (BIOs). Greenpeace, Habitat for Humanity, and the Red Cross are well-known examples. NGOs are non-profit and generally private. Some are international, while others are national or local in focus. According to the Union of International Associations, by 2004 there were nearly 6,600 non-governmental organizations in existence (1). The attention and active care that they offer usually centers around a few archetypal themes: human rights, animals and the environment, developing the third world, women's issues, conflict resolution, and the promotion of peace. They can range in size and scope from a local after-school program for at-risk kids to Amnesty International with almost three million members in 150 countries or the United Nations, which, with its considerable power and an almost 200-nation membership, is the largest international benevolent organization in the planet's history.

Most BIOs began as an outcry against suffering or injustice. The International Red Cross was begun by Henri Dunant, a Swiss merchant banker who followed Napoleon III onto the battlefield to get his approval for a business deal (2). The unequaled carnage that he witnessed prompted him to organize local residents to pull dead bodies off the battle field. He went on to devote himself to stopping and assuaging the atrocities of war. OXFAM, a giant international aid organization, was initiated in WWII when British citizens established the Oxford Committee for Famine Relief. It came to be known by the organization's telegraph address – "Oxfam." The International Voluntary Service, also a response to war, was established in the wake of World War I in Europe.

The Sierra Club's 700,000 members owe their allegiance to the club's founder, John Muir, who was a passionate and renowned conservationist and environmentalist in the early 20th century. This organization was once cited as "the most effective of the conservation groups" by political scientist Grant McConnell (3). Many philanthropic groups began in order to provide immediate assistance in times of war, famine, or conflict, but they soon saw that focusing their efforts at the cause of these societal ills would offer a much more lasting effect for these affected regions. This is when many organizations expanded from providing food, shelter, and medical attention to the broader issues of human rights, environmental protection, and peace-building.

To achieve their philanthropic ends, benevolent international organizations employ government lobbying, litigation, extensive scientific research, grassroots networking, and education at home and abroad. In order to function optimally, BIOs must operate in union and collaboration with governmental organizations, the scientific community, big business, and local individuals. These eclectic collaborations were termed "trans-national advocacy networks" in the seminal work *Activists Beyond Borders* by Margaret Keck and Kathryn Sikkinik. A perfect example of this is found in the development of a highway system in the Brazilian state of Rondonia. The team enlisted to bring the project to fruition includes U.S. human rights and environmental NGOs, Brazilian anthropologists, World Bank environmental staff and consultants, US congressional representatives, and media correspondents in the field of international environmentalism (4).

Many of these altruistic organizations whose physical scope does not extend beyond their national boundaries deal with issues that are nonetheless international -- the environment, crisis aid, and human rights. Very few of these organizations, if any, push nationalistic agendas. The precedent for BIOs was set centuries ago by the Catholic church in Europe and Buddhism in Asia. These institutions had considerable power and wealth and used much of it to ease suffering and hardship among their followers (5). The concept of tithing laid an important foundation for all charitable donations today which are the fuel for countless humanitarian efforts. The Salvation Army actually began as a religious crusade, but found that people could not receive messages of spirituality if their basic needs were not met first. It has since become one of the largest benevolent organizations in the U.S; the Salvation Army senior program alone serves 25,000 clients annually (6).

Many landmark events and important movements in history were sourced in BIO, or NGO, activity and ideology: the 1833-65 anti-slavery movement in the United States, the Geneva Conventions of 1864, the international Slavery Convention of 1926, and the 1920-23 campaign by missionaries and colonialists to end female circumcision in Kenya (7).

International aid in the form of money and resources has traditionally been left up to national governments and their en masse efforts to balance out the global wealth gradient. However, the arrival and maturation of sizeable BIOs in recent decades now provides a necessary intermediary between these lump-sum flows of cash and their recipients. Larger BIOs such as the International Red Cross and Amnesty International have the staff and global ubiquity to absorb and effectively utilize large sums of money from government sources. Smaller BIOs are often funded by these mega-organizations to implement more localized, personal-scale distribution of these funds. Their local presence and grassroots connection to communities posits them as ideal husbanders of these beneficial funds and resources.

Enthusiastic participation from local indigenous populations, relief workers observe, is critical to the success of any aid program. Cultivating support from individual donors at home and generating participation from locals at the relief site are both essential to the overall recovery plight. One group that has immense untapped power and potential is the female population of these regions (8). The latent labor and intellectual power of women is an unequaled resource in the developing world. Salient NGOs that focus on women are the Global Fund for Women, WEDO (Women's Empowerment and Development Organization), and NOW (National Organization for Women).

Former President Bill Clinton's "Clinton Global Initiative" displays a demonstrable focus on women, and more broadly it has proven very effectual by bringing together powerful and divergent elements of society. By uniting prominent CEOs, philanthropists (including fourteen Nobel laureates), NGO and government leaders, and significant members of the media, this organization has raised $57 billion and reached 200 million people in 150 countries (9). It is currently setting up health clinics in Africa and also focusing on the needs of women and girls, especially victims of sex trafficking. In interviews, Mr. Clinton speaks very eloquently about the connection between educating and empowering women and the resultant reduction in poverty and decrease in population growth rates in a society (10). His organization was also, incidentally, giving significant attention and aid to Haiti well before the catastrophic earthquake of 2010. The former president and first lady actually honeymooned in Haiti, so his love for the country is of long standing.

Representing a completely new avenue for benevolent projects, famous TV chef Jamie Oliver's *Food Revolution* is a weekly televised show which documents Jamie's efforts to change America's poor eating habits. He focuses on changing the daily menus in the schools in Huntington, West Virginia, a city which he identified as having one of the nation's worst overall diets. Jamie's desire to help incite positive change in the health of the American people is obvious, earnest, and overflowing, and his impossible-not-to-like demeanor couples powerfully with this unique media platform.

One innovation in the way that resources are delivered by NGOs to potential recipients is through "microcredit" low-interest loans to farmers and business people in the developing world. The average loan size in 2000 in Honduras, for example, was only $129 U.S. This prevalent mechanism for spurring economic growth is said to reach more than 25% of the applicable market in thirteen Latin American countries (11). The 2006 Nobel Peace Prize was given to Bangladeshi economist Muhammad Yunus for his revolutionary work with microcredit loans that centered on women as recipients. Many philanthropic organizations also receive funding from charitable foundations and from contracts for specific tasks from governmental programs or bodies such as the UN. BIOs of all sizes, however, receive the majority of their funding from private individuals who simply write a check for their favorite cause. This is the most direct pathway for funds to flow from wealthy nations and individuals to poorer ones (12). In 2003, individuals in the United States donated over $200 billion to charitable organizations (13).

The total number of NGOs registered with the United Nations rose from forty in the 1940s to 2,614 in 2005 (14). The interaction between the UN and non-governmental organizations has been critical for both players. The UN began as a peace-keeping body designed to intervene in conflicts and advocate peace, but they had little power to execute, implement, and maintain their accords. This power to implement came with the UN peace-keeping troops and with NGO ground involvement. In 1956, UN Secretary General Dag Hammarskjold spoke to a group in New York City about the link between cultivating peace and protecting human rights. Even though there were no human rights treaties in existence at that time, he pushed for human rights promotion and international legislation. Cultivating peace and protecting human rights were soon found to be inseparable pursuits. He urged NGOs to join him in this fight and to investigate and record human rights violations the world over (15).

In Hammarskjold's honor, the UN created the position of High Commissioner for Human Rights in 1993. Today NGOs are an invaluable part of the UN body of international action. The UN is the largest and most powerful international organization in history, so its direction and leadership are of the utmost importance. The United States has considerable influence with the UN; some countries would argue that the U.S. has *too* much influence. Therefore, it is critical that the United States recognizes its power over this world-leading benevolent body and acquiesce to some degree to its universal philanthropic agenda. This will require that the U.S. yields more often to utilitarian economics, but in doing this we will soon see that lifting up other nations can only lift us in return.

Some evidence of U.S. philanthropy was seen when U.S. Assistant Secretary of State for democracy, human rights, and labor, Lorne W. Craner, recently outlined U.S. efforts to spread democracy and ameliorate human life in the Middle East, central Asia, and China. We as a nation have also recently created the "Five billion dollar millennium challenge account" which offers money to nations who show attempts to reform their economic, social, and political operations.

A few sobering statistics describing our modern globe, mentioned earlier, make it obvious that large and effective BIOs are needed. 800 million people suffer from malnutrition on the globe. 900 million people are illiterate. Over one billion live on less than two dollars a day. Perhaps one-fourth of humanity lives in poverty. Organizations that are combating these bleak statistics are groups such as: Human Rights Watch, CARE international, UNICEF, OXFAM international, and the Federation Internationale des Droits de l'Homme (FIDH). In the environmental realm, while 1.7 million species of plants and animals are known to exist, we lose approximately 50,000 a year due to deforestation and global warming. However, it is estimated that there may be as many as three to fifty million total species in existence, which would mean that proportionally we would be losing from 100,000 to 1.5 million species per year on the planet (16). Some agencies that are combating this loss are the Friends of the Earth International, Greenpeace, the World Wildlife Fund, and the Sierra Club.

Some larger NGOs such as the World Bank and the World Trade Organization have policies which help the flow of capital and positively affect the developing world. Yet many of their missions also have motives which are self-serving for powerful groups or governments in the first world. Overhauling or a supervised restructuring of these organizations may be beneficial. Worth mentioning, several businesses in the Western world have decidedly philanthropic piths which are guided by the ethos of the company. Chick-Fil-A, for instance, is owned by a man who is a dedicated Christian, so the branches are closed on Sunday and the company funds religious organizations and NGOs. Also, Home Depot's founder believes in the entrepreneurial spirit and funds fledgling business in the developing world (17).

In fact, there are currently over 2,000 U.S. corporations with foundations that are focused on philanthropic giving. According to Ari Weinberg's August, 2003, *Forbes* article, "America's Most Generous Corporations," Target, Wal-Mart, and Ford each donate over 100 million a year to charitable causes, while Albertson's and Best Buy both give away approximately two percent of their total annual income (18).

Amnesty International (A.I.) also gives, but on the fronts of social justice. A.I. has 2.8 million members and supporters in 150 countries, and they fight quite effectively for human rights around the globe. During the late 1990s, Amnesty International's secretary general had written indelibly on the whiteboard in her office: "advocacy, not impartiality" (19). This attitude is evidenced in the 2005 claim by the organization that Guantanamo (US Marine base in Cuba) was a "gulag," which prompted Secretary of Defense Donald Rumsfeld to respond and defend the White House publicly. The fact that it generated a public response from the U.S. government shows that it struck a chord of truth, and that A.I. has enough credibility to be taken seriously on these issues. It also displays that NGOs are not pushovers, and that they add some teeth to the larger benevolent movement.

In this light, the international NGO body can be compared to the ancient mythical chimera – a beast fused from three other animals. The body of the NGO chimera is the humanitarian aid and localized infrastructural development, the brains are its ability to research, educate, lobby government, and shape international policy, while the teeth of the NGO beast are displayed in the direct challenging of existing regimes through protest, sanctions, and media exposure.

The size, power, ubiquity, and effectiveness of benevolent international organizations is impressive and growing. Many magnanimous individuals and groups have brought these agencies into existence and allowed them to evolve and prosper. They are particularly important and well-suited to this modern international scene because they are flexible, broad-based, and often multi-national. They are an immediate and tangible beacon of compassion for those who are desperate, in need, and powerless. Where governments or charitable foundations may delay in delivering rapid, visceral help, BIOs rush in to help with established and personal networks in needy regions and communities. NGOs give a man a fish *and* a fishing pole. On the other side of this battle, NGOs are at the helm in providing, to governments and the general public alike, the necessary research and information about pervasive injustices and human suffering on the planet. This spread of information is perhaps the most critical element in alleviating the abuse of our environment and of our fellow man because awareness is the beginning of healing, and it is the most powerful remedy for any evil.

In 1998, Pierre Sane gave a prophetic statement about Amnesty International which goes far to disclose the true nature of NGOs collectively and paints a positive future for the emerging benevolent nature of human interaction:

"Amnesty International was not established to free prisoners of conscience. Amnesty was established to contribute to the full realization of Human Rights for all." And the spirit behind the organization is "the benevolent influence of a universal, uniting, indomitable power usually referred to as compassion" (20).

The Fourth Way to Save the Planet

Uplift Women: Women are heavily repressed
in much of the developing world, which denies them
basic rights and cripples their societies' development.
Women's ability to be educated, vote, and own
property has myriad positive effects on a society
including reduction in birth rates, child mortality, and
domestic abuse, as well as an increase in literacy (2).
The feminine perspective and presence at all levels
of society is critical for the planet to move forward in
its evolution. This inevitable rebalancing of our very
human nature – within every person and every nation
-- entails less focus on aggression and domination and
more espousal of compassion, communication, and
interdependence. We must hold our women on high
and encourage our daughters to be leaders of the next
generation. Salient organizations that support women are
UNICEF, Women For Women International, and CARE.
Engaging and supporting the essence and power of
women will highlight and cultivate the grandest version
of humanity's future.

The Rise of Women

In 1959, Senator John F. Kennedy agreed to support a program which would bring hundreds of top Kenyan scholars to universities in the United States. Funded through the Joseph P. Kennedy, Jr. foundation, this program, which came to be known as "Airlift Africa," brought around 300 Kenyans to study in the U.S. One of those students was a young woman named Wangari Maathai who went on to earn her bachelor's degree from Mt. Scholastica College in Kansas and her Masters from the University of Pittsburgh. But she did not stop there. Eventually Wangari completed her doctoral studies in veterinary biology and thus became the first east African woman ever to receive a Ph.D. In the late 1970s, Professor Maathai founded the Green Belt Movement which focused on women's rights, anti-poverty efforts, and environmentalism. One tangible product of the movement was the successful planting of forty million trees in the East African region.

Despite sexist and prejudiced hurdles along the way in her home nation of Kenya, her altruistic efforts earned Wangari Maathai the 2004 Nobel Peace Prize. Thus, after receiving a helping hand from a forward-thinking senator Kennedy, this amazing woman went on to set precedents and crash through barriers that would improve the East African environment and social structure forever.

Professor Maathai of Kenya is an example of how the rise of one woman can lift up a community, a nation, and an entire region. The world is at a turning point where more emphasis on female guidance, skills, belief systems, and ethos are essential for us to move through our current problems and onto a higher level of functioning. Energetically, it will behoove many governments, corporations, and leaders to come to balance by complementing sometimes excessive "yang" aggressive and dominant energy with more "yin" communicative and collaborative energy. Yet the foundation of this shift is centered on women themselves, because in most of the world females are still second class citizens in several clearly measurable, very real ways.

Women own a paltry one percent of the land on the planet (2). Eighty million fewer females than males are currently enrolled in school across the globe, and even in the most progressive industrialized countries, women are far from income parity in the job market (3). In every nation but one, women could not vote until the 20th century (4), and in several Middle Eastern countries, women still have only partial voting rights or none at all. Most shocking is that one in three women on the planet are raped or physically beaten within their lifetime (5). In fact, more women die from domestic violence than from war, traffic accidents, malaria, and cancer combined (6).

The economic marginalization of women, it could be said, is as important and deleterious as any other form of repression. According to the UN, women earn only 10% of the world's income (7). This is true despite the fact that in most cultures women perform the majority of household and childrearing duties, and in the developing world, women are responsible for up to 80% of local food production (8). In the poorest nations where household chores include collecting firewood and water, women and children spend inordinate amounts of time on these rudimentary tasks every day. This often precludes children's attendance in school and prohibits mothers from seeking employment outside the home. Yet, this puts women in intimate contact with the Earth and its resources and posits them in a perfect position to advise the management of these resources at the local and national levels. In the developed or first world, dual-income households with children also often see mothers working full-time and silently taking responsibility for a larger share of raising the children in an unspoken contract that gender-divides labor. In short, women are vastly productive and yet substantially underpaid.

As of 2008, census data shows that full-time employed women earn 77.8% as much as full-time employed men in the United States. The average income was $35,102 for women and $45,113 for men. African-American women in the U.S. in 2008 earned $31,009, Latina women earned $26,612, and Asian women made $ 40,374 (9). In most European countries, women earn between 70 - 85% of what men earn, with women in Luxembourg and Ireland at the top of the list. These gaps were found to be much wider in the Asian nations of Japan, Republic of Korea, Malaysia, Singapore, the Philippines, China, Thailand, and Vietnam. The former four nations demonstrated the most egregious disparity, with women earning approximately half that of men (10).

Janet Momsen points to three disadvantages that women have in the labor market. One, women are excluded from many types of employment, usually based on a lack of facilities for women or a perception of "physical weakness." Two, women are often concentrated in the periphery of the labor market in the informal sector, which is very insecure. Three, heavily female-dominated jobs (such as nurse, secretary, and school teacher) become categorically devalued and hence of less earning power (11).

Education is perhaps the most important tool for ensuring the rise of women, especially those who are poor or disenfranchised. Across the planet, tens of millions of fewer girls are enrolled in school than boys (12), resulting in the fact that 64% of all illiterate adults are women (13). These statistics are due to myriad factors including disenfranchisement, lack of basic rights, male-dominated societies, and simply the burden of child rearing and household management -- all of which lessen women's access to education. In most of the developing world at the primary school level, near gender parity has been achieved, yet in Africa, the Middle East, and South Asia, boys still predominate (14). At the high school level in the developing world, the gender gap widens, with over half of girls not attending school in west and central Africa and 15% not attending in Latin America (15). The number of men in college in the developing world nearly doubles that of women (16). Of particular note is that in industrialized countries, the story is quite different; approximately equal numbers of males and females attend school at all levels, except in universities where females are more present (17). In fact, 58% of all bachelors and masters degrees in the U.S. in 2006 were awarded to women (18).

A plethora of studies link the education of women with positive effects on their lives, on their families, and on the world. Educating women both empowers them to rise above repressive settings and it also tends to diminish their fertility rates in regions of the world where the population explosion is a critical problem. Across the developing world, every 10% that the female literacy rate increases, the total fertility rate decreases by about one-half child per woman, which is very significant (19).

A woman's ability to read is statistically linked to six important indicators. First, literate women tend to marry later than illiterate women. Second, once married, they are more likely to matriculate their children into school. Attending school lowers the labor value of children, and hence women feel less motivated to have several children (20). Third, educated women also more frequently enter the paid labor force, increasing their decision-making power in the home (21). Fourth, literate women understand health and hygiene better, so more of their children tend to survive, and hence fewer children overall need to be born (22). Moreover, women who can read are more likely to be knowledgeable about family planning. Lastly, literate women have more social and public interaction outside the immediate family which broadens their support networks and lessens the desire to have multiple children (23).

Three Cups of Tea author Greg Mortenson states that when you educate a man, you educate one person, but when you educate a woman, you educate a whole family. This is because women tend to teach their offspring to read. A salient example of female literacy being linked to positive societal ramifications is in the Indian state of Kerala. The state has below-average per capita income, yet displays markedly higher life expectancy of both males and females than the national average (approximately ten years above the national average for both men and women) (24). This has been connected to the fact that literacy programs, especially those for women, have been steadily supported and implemented there since the early 1800s (25). The women-to-men ratio in Kerala is also much higher than the national average at 104/100, compared to 93/100 in India at large. Moreover, much of the community (the Nairs) is guided by a matrilineal land and property inheritance, and women in the region are often known to work for pay (26).

The debate over the relative strengths and weaknesses of men as compared to women has existed for millennia. And despite sharing over 99% of their genetic code, men and women do have quantifiable physical differences. Men, for instance, are usually physically larger and stronger, while women mature measurably faster than men, based on hormonal and brain activity. More specifically, the prefrontal cortex, which guides and controls emotions, is larger and matures more rapidly in women, while the anterior cingulated cortex, which weighs options and assesses decisions, is also larger in females (27). Physical strength and aggression translated to security and prosperity for millennia. But today, when reason, wise decision-making, and productive management of one's emotions are critical capacities for CEOs, diplomats, and leaders, women are shining more brightly, and more often stepping into the lead role.

Women are indeed rising up on many social levels and helping to steer the globe into this next century. In the 1990s, twenty-five women were president or prime minister of their country, and today prominent nations such as South Africa, Switzerland, Argentina, and India all have female presidents (28). Also, as of 2007, 17% of parliament members worldwide were women, and women comprise 18% of the U.S. Congress (29). The global social and political climate seems to be calling forth and supporting a different style of aegis which favors women leaders.

In 1990, Eagley and Johnson researched the results of over 150 studies from around the globe which tried to explain the fundamental differences in male and female leadership styles. In general, men were found to lead with a "transactional" style which focuses on delegating tasks to subordinates and rewarding compliance with money in a contractual exchange. Aggression, domination, and the use of force elicit success in such a system (30). Women were found to lead in a "transformational" style that highlights interpersonal relationships, inspiration, and uplifting feedback (31). Most importantly, women were "less concerned with personal power and more concerned with the organization as a whole" (32).

After their exhaustive examination of these numerous studies, Eagley and Johnson found that leaders of differing gender did not differ in their effectiveness, rather that one style of leadership is often more effective for a certain population or a certain national dynamic than another.

One paramount struggle that all global leaders are facing amidst the current economic downturn is the need to protect the environment while extending basic rights and services to over a billion people on the planet who currently do not possess them. Often pure capitalists see these processes as mutually exclusive or even contrary, but authors Gita Sen, Adrienne Germain and Lincoln Chen warn against this.

"Approaches to economic growth and ecological sustainability must be such as to secure livelihoods, basic needs, political participation, and women's reproductive rights, not to work against them. Thus, environmental policies and programs must support and sustain livelihoods and basic needs, not counterpose "nature" against the survival needs of the most vulnerable people in the present" (33).

Indeed we must not see caring for the environment and for basic rights of women, for instance, as adversely affecting economic factors. In fact, engaging more full participation of women as contributors to national governments and economies will help disclose that the endeavors of economic advancement, caring for the environment, and social justice are mutually supportive. In the words of Mahatma Gandhi,

"If only the women of the world came together, they could display such heroic nonviolence as to kick away the atom bomb like a mere ball. If the women of Asia wake up they will dazzle the world. My experiment in nonviolence would be instantly successful if I could secure women's help" (34).

Taking a more capital-driven approach, since 1944, supranational institutions such as the International Monetary Fund (IMF) and World Bank have been attempting to ameliorate economic conditions in the world's poorer nations by lending them large sums of money. Though this lending has improved economic indices in many countries, critics say that these institutions' motives are mixed. By late 1993, thirty-five of forty-six African countries had adopted IMF and World Bank "structural adjustment programs" which must be implemented as contingencies for receiving a loan (35). The overall impetus behind these programs is dubious when one examines the widespread results that the programs bring about. Structural Adjustment Programs (SAP) essentially shift production from being domestically focused (trade of goods and services within a country) to being internationally focused (exported goods).

The work of women is therefore instantly devalued because they do the lion's share of domestic, unskilled, and untradeable labor. These SAP policies also pull huge monies out of public services such as education, infrastructure development, and health care, and put it toward neo-colonial resource extraction and export-focused production. This directly and negatively affects those dependent on public services, especially women. Many health care systems have become largely privatized, as in the case of Nigeria, which is now fee-for-service (36). This has a huge negative impact on the availability and quality of reproductive and child-rearing care for women.

Malaak Compton-Rock, wife of comedian Chris Rock, is using her celebrity to bring awareness and relief to issues affecting women and children. As the daughter of an activist mother, Malaak has spent years working closely with UNICEF, and she has also authored the book, *If It Takes a Village, Build One.* She has personally taken underprivileged teens from New York to South African slums to foster communication and to plant a philanthropic seed in American youths. She recently appeared on the Oprah Winfrey show to promote the "Product (Red)" Campaign which partners with American Express, Apple, Starbucks, and the Gap, among many other companies, to donate part of their proceeds to the Global Fund in order to fight poverty and AIDS in Africa.

Denizens of the beleaguered nation of Haiti also have a well-publicized plight, but the struggles of their women are perhaps even more delineated. American actress and altruist Maria Bello is doing something to change this. Formerly working with "Save the Children" to help young people around the planet, Maria has also established her own women's organization which is focusing on improving access to health care, education, and jobs for women in Haiti. Notably, Maria began her work in Haiti long before the devastating earthquake of 2010.

Reproductive health is another aspect of women's lives on this planet that offers some sobering statistics. Approximately half a million women die annually in the developing world from childbirth-related issues. That is one death every minute. Two-thirds of those deaths occur in Subsaharan Africa, and most of the remainder occur in India (37). In fact, over a lifetime, a woman's chance of dying during childbirth in Subsaharan Africa is 1 in 22, as opposed to 1 in 8,000 in industrialized countries (38). This means that in most of Africa, a woman having a baby has only slightly better chances of surviving than if she played Russian roulette with a loaded gun.

A woman's access to reproductive health care and contraception is essential to building healthy communities and nations. This access is often limited by strongly paternalistic societies or living situations (39)(40). Even age-old traditions such as arranged marriage can affect a woman's health. Over sixty million women alive today worldwide have had an arranged marriage, and these women tend to marry younger and hence have children at a younger age (41). One simple fact makes this pertinent -- women under the age of fifteen who have children are five times more likely to die in childbirth than women in their twenties (42). Therefore, allowing women to mature and "come of age" a bit more before marriage and childbirth has many statistical benefits.

Religion can also be a hindrance to women's control over their own health and reproduction. Author Aziza Ahmed writes about the irony of fierce opposition to U.S. military aggression by Islamic countries yet an alignment with that aggression if it is directed against women. "While the world's citizens struggle against such demonstrations of (U.S. military) power, other conservative forces and nations, including the Vatican and Islamic countries, are able to merge their own agendas with that of the U.S. government's; ironically, they are all allies in the war against women" (43). While I see the U.S. government as relatively pro-woman when situated in the global political context, Ahmed's religious critique comes not without anecdotal foundation. In 2004, for instance, three Catholic bishops in the United States openly declared that no politicians who support a woman's right to terminate her pregnancy could receive communion from them (44).

Pope Benedict XVI has said that Africa's AIDS problem will not be solved by condoms, but in fact, exacerbated by them (45). Yet only 23% of couples in Subsaharan Africa use contraception, as compared to 61% in the developing world in general and 79% in East Asia and the Pacific (46). It is no surprise then that two-thirds of all HIV cases, and a full 75% of all women on Earth who are HIV positive are found in Subsaharan Africa (47). Something that is indeed exacerbating this problem is that among 15 to 24-year-olds in low-to-middle income nations, less than one-fourth have "comprehensive and correct" knowledge about HIV (48). UNICEF and other organizations have been remedying this dearth of HIV education quite rapidly over the past five to eight years, which is an encouraging trend.

The Beijing Platform of Action of the Fourth World Conference on Women in 1995 defined the foundational principles of sexual rights thusly: "The human rights of women include their right to have control over and decide freely and responsibly on matters related to their sexuality, including sexual and reproductive health, free of coercion, discrimination and violence" (49).

Perhaps surprisingly, sexual abuse – including rape -- by one's regular sexual partner is much more common than sexual abuse by acquaintances or others. This was ascertained by a study which investigated sexual violence against women in ten countries around the globe (50). The percentage of women who had experienced sexual abuse from their partner was 59% in Ethiopia, 30% in Thailand, 14% in Brazil, and 6% in Japan. With non-intimate partners, the rates were significantly lower, ranging from 12% to 1% among all nations surveyed.

Rape is also a common tool used during wartime for demoralization, abuse of power, and genetic fragmentation of a rival ethnic group. This has occurred throughout history, but very prevalently in the recent conflicts in Bosnia and Herzegovina, the 1971 Bangladeshi struggle for independence, and several civil wars in Africa. The extent of this atrocious practice is overwhelming when actual wartime statistics are presented. In the war in Bosnia and Herzegovina, between 30,000 and 50,000 women were raped (51). In Bangladesh's 1971 war for independence, from 250,000 to 400,000 women were raped, producing approximately 25,000 pregnancies (52). Around this same number, perhaps as many as half a million women, were raped during the 1994 genocide in Rwanda (53).

An entire chapter is devoted to the deleterious trend of sex trafficking earlier in this book, but one positive story requires mention here. Mu Sochua, Cambodia's former Minister of Women's and Veteran's affairs, is fighting sex trafficking by attempting to persuade poor villagers to cease selling their daughters into the trade. In this unique approach, Sochua has implemented massive ideological media campaigns that promote the intrinsic value and quality of women and young girls. She modified a common Cambodian adage from "A man is gold, a woman is a white piece of cloth" to "Men are gold, women are precious gems" (54). With parental support, Ms. Sochua estimates that she recovers about ten percent of girls who were originally sold into the local sex trade (55). Another positive note was the enactment of the International Criminal Court "Rome Statute." The law is a very powerful protection ensuring that cases of sexual abuse and rape get appropriate attention and do get tried and prosecuted. The statute fights against sex trafficking and female circumcision, as well.

Despite the above staggering numbers, the most common form of violence against women is domestic violence, which usually takes the form of verbal and physical abuse. In a survey conducted in households in fifty-seven countries, half of women aged fifteen to forty-nine said a husband or partner is justified in beating his wife under certain circumstances (56). The percentage of women that agreed with that statement varied widely across nations, including 89% agreement in Mali, 59% in Iraq, 39% in Turkey, 24% in the Philippines, and 6% in Jamaica (57).

Not all extraordinary women help by feeding the hungry or fighting for human rights. And all who change the world have not attained celebrity status. Some simply lead exemplary lives. Joanna Medawar Nachef of Los Angeles, California, is one such woman whose musical prowess and personal gravitas are making the world a better place. An immigrant from Lebanon, Joanna earned her doctorate in music from the University of Southern California and now conducts several choirs in the L.A. area, including the Los Cancioneros Master Chorale. With two children, a loving husband, a thriving career in music, and a cosmopolitan flair, this always exquisitely dressed director is every bit as much mother as diva. Her ability to speak perfect French, Arabic, and English has led to her appointment with the U.S. Department of State as a liaison encouraging musical and cultural exchange with Lebanon. Moreover, she has several times brought her choirs, including her student choirs from El Camino College, to sing in Carnegie Hall in New York City. On her fifth and most recent Carnegie Hall appearance, she directed a choir from her native Lebanon which she blended with her singers from the U.S. Joanna's passion, grace, and panache make her stand out as a woman and as a human being. She elevates those around her and reminds us of how grand, dynamic, and fulfilling our lives can be.

We must support our women because the women in our lives are forever supporting us. Mothers are always in the process of raising the next generation of the world's children, both boys and girls. Moreover, and contrary to popular belief, women are often the primary economic contributors to the family, especially in cases of single parenthood and divorce in the developed world, polygamy in Africa, and widowhood in South Asia (58). Moreover, women have been shown to spend a larger percentage of their income than men directly on the family's children (59). Yet with dramatically less earning power and less ownership of land and resources, women's ability to care for children is handicapped.

Organizations such as the Global Fund for Women, UNICEF, CARE, Amnesty International, Womankind Worldwide, Women for Women International, and UNIFEM (United Nations Development Fund for Women) are powerful international forces that are shifting many of these statistics for the better. These organizations work very successfully on improving women's access to education, health care, and political rights, especially in poorer countries. Supporting these groups is an excellent way to immediately and directly help the plight of women throughout the world.

In the wealthier nations, we can raise our girls to believe that they can and will be the leaders of the future. We should encourage them to stand out, speak up, and make their presence known at every level -- from the local to the international. Women in the developed world have immense power compared to their counterparts in still developing nations, so their full utilization and engagement in the world's paramount economic, political, and environmental issues is absolutely critical to the planet's well-being, and to the rise of women the world over.

The Fifth Way to Save the Planet

Make Your Household Efficient: In the

West, indulgent consumption is at the root of our biggest problems. Trash production, wasting food, and overuse of energy are pervasive vices, and these are all centered at home. The average American uses twice the energy of the average European, while Europe uses nearly twice as much energy per capita as China, and four times as much as India. Moreover, domestic water consumption per household in the U.S. is 145 gallons per day, compared to 72 gallons per day in France and 8 gallons per day in Nigeria (3). Americans also consume the most gasoline and food on the planet. An earnest commitment to conservation and more efficient living within the most wasteful countries is of the highest importance and very attainable. Unbridled consumption without responsibility is simply unsustainable since we are already over-burdening the carrying capacity of the Earth and its resources. Our consumption, when focused wisely, can actually be a powerful solution in that it funds industries and companies that are moving the globe in the right direction.

Living More Efficiently

"When I give food to the poor, they call me a saint. When I ask why the poor have no food, they call me a communist."

- Archbishop Dom Helder Camara of Brazil

"Living in this world and not being an environmentalist is like living on a boat in a stormy sea and not having the skills of a sailor."

- Gregory J. Schwartz

I had a dream the other night that I was hungry but I found there was no food in my cupboards or refrigerator. Then I went to the grocery store and saw that the shelves were completely bare. The sinking realization came over me that there was no food to be found in my entire city of Los Angeles. Day after day in this excruciatingly long dream, I had to watch my wife and child, as well as my neighbors, starving to death in front of my eyes. Other essentials were also hard to come by. Our only source of water was a polluted river about two miles from our house. Since everyone was sharing this river, even for laundry and bathing, drinking from it was ill-advised, but it was unfortunately our only choice. Thousands of people in the city died every day, but still nothing changed and no help came. I cannot describe the unshakeable helplessness that I felt.

The one curious twist in the dream was that we still could watch television. Each day, our predicament became harder to bear as we sat and watched news and shows from around the world picturing people living in such abundance and luxury. They looked so happy and carefree. I wondered how they could live like that while knowing what we were experiencing in L.A.

"Some care, and they do help," said my next-door neighbor, "but most don't. That's just the way it is."

The most frightening part of my dream was that when I awakened, it was real. Not for me, but for 800 million people on the planet, this nightmare is their daily life. If you live in a wealthy nation, even if you don't want it, you have a small part of the responsibility to make life better for those who are so terribly suffering elsewhere on the planet. Each of the "five ways to save the planet" has ripple effects that produce positive global ramifications in countless interconnected ways. Using renewable energy, eating organic food, supporting the rise of women in the developing world, and giving money to benevolent organizations are powerful and focused ways to help. Below, I discuss how managing our households more efficiently will allow us to see how surprisingly imbalanced and wasteful the world's use of natural resources truly is. And finally, in that awareness, we can collectively decide that no one should excessively abuse our resources, nor should anyone perish from lack of them.

Currently, a large portion of the planet's people are living quite inefficiently, and the effects are showing up in some unexpected and undesirable ways. A few icons of human development are large enough to be visible from outer space including the Egyptian pyramids at Giza, the Great Wall of China, and the Fresh Kills Landfill on the southern edge of New York City (1). That is, from a distance, what is now notable about this planet is the sheer accumulation of waste. Specifically, residents of the United States generate 500 billion pounds of trash per year. Consumption is king in the wealthy nations of the world. It is the root of our biggest environmental, financial, and health-related problems, and it also has the power to be the source of countless solutions.

Citizens of most of Europe, Canada, Japan, New Zealand, Australia, oil producing nations of the Middle East, and the United States consume resources at exorbitant rates compared to poorer nations. We consume food, energy, water, wood, fossil fuels, and products manufactured around the globe, including, of note, recreational drugs - all at levels never before seen on Earth. Our buying and usage habits have created a global environmental crisis both directly, through fossil fuel burning, and indirectly, through buying products that necessitate deforestation such as beef and tropical hardwoods. Also, especially in America, our fixation on food is a significant contributor to very high cancer, diabetes, and obesity rates. The powerful thing about our copious consumption is that it wields much influence over markets, industries, resource supplies, and our own health. Because of this, redirecting our consumption will indeed prove to be the source of our most effective environmental and health solutions. In wealthy nations, we vote with our dollars, and by buying environmentally-friendly products and foods, we effectively choose which companies and practices flourish or flounder. In this chapter, I will look at how the developed world deals with water, energy, food, and trash.

One essential commodity that needs to be conscientiously managed on the planet is food. Being more efficient and aware in the way that we deal with food, in the Western world especially, will help us and our poorer neighbors immensely. About 65% of Americans are overweight, while a full one-third are clinically obese, and that figure includes children. In Europe, the total percentage overweight is usually between thirty and forty percent of the population, while obesity rates normally hover between ten and twenty percent. Numbers in Asia and Africa are much lower, yet rising, especially in wealthy urban settings. This widespread obesity is particularly notable when we consider that elsewhere on this same planet, just over one billion people (one-seventh of the planet) are malnourished to the point that 100,000 die daily from starvation or starvation-related conditions (2). Said another way, while much of the world is dying from gluttonous food consumption and its related diseases of diabetes, cancer, and atherosclerosis, another sizeable portion of the world is expiring by the millions due to an acute lack of nourishment.

Obesity costs the U.S. health care system between $200 billion and $340 billion annually, depending on how totals are generated (3). Yet, based on estimates from USAID (United States agency for international development), UNFAO (United Nations Food and Agriculture Organization), and the World Food Programme, it will only cost between five and six billion dollars per year to provide one daily meal to the approximately one billion undernourished people on the planet right now (4). Clearly the resources are available to correct this imbalance. If we ate less in the U.S. and saved 20% of our health costs related to obesity for a single year – conservatively, $40 billion – that would be enough to sustain all of the hungry people on the planet several times over. To go beyond sustenance and supply a full, balanced diet to this hungry billion people, estimates are closer to $50 billion per year, yet still a modest savings in health care by eating less in the U.S. alone nearly covers the entire tab.

By solving one problem, the other is also ameliorated. By dealing with food consumption more efficiently and reasonably at home, we can solve food problems abroad as well. If citizens of wealthy nations decrease their life-threatening habits such as over-eating and smoking, to mention another, the amount of money that we save on hospitalization could bring hundreds of millions of people overseas from the brink of starvation to a life of some dignity and satisfaction. Approximately $10 billion is spent in the U.S. every year on advertising for cigarettes (5). According to estimates by the organizations above, that amount would provide more than enough food to keep every starving person on the planet alive for an entire year.

This issue of dealing with food more efficiently has other layers as well. The American Association for the Advancement of Science states that 78% of the world's malnourished children live inside countries which actually have food surpluses (6). Eleven countries in Sub-Saharan Africa are net food exporters while over 200 million people in the region are drastically under-nourished (7). Even during the severe droughts of the late 70s and early 80s, food was exported from the most ravaged countries in the desertified Sahel region of Africa. Moreover, in India in 1995, again over 200 million people were essentially starving, yet the nation exported $625 million worth of wheat and flour, and $1.3 billion worth of rice (8).

Many of these countries are determined to earn foreign capital, achieve a favorable balance of trade, and get out of debt, so selling food on the international market is more attractive than feeding it to their own people. This approach is condoned by loan contingencies imposed upon these nations. These policies force destitute nations to cut off services and funding to their own underserved citizenry in favor of producing cash crops and manufactured products for export. This mimics the exploitative tactics utilized by colonial powers in the 18th and 19th centuries.

George McGovern, a one-time candidate for U.S. President, was appointed by President John F. Kennedy in

1961 to head the U.S. Food for Peace Program. Then and now, Mr. McGovern sees one specific program – school lunches – as critical to the development of the poorest nations. Malnourished children do not have the energy or means to attend school and succeed. A free school lunch has been shown to dramatically increase school attendance and academic performance (9). This tackles two huge problems, illiteracy and malnutrition, at the same time, and reinforces the truth that they are intimately tied together. Indeed, the first two of eight Millennium Development goals, created at a special session of the UN in 2000, are to "Eradicate hunger and extreme poverty" and "Achieve universal primary education" by the year 2015.

Looking at the global food equation from a broad perspective, another point calls for discussion, and that is beef. Beef is a staple in the American and European diets, and increasingly so in Asia and among the nouveau riche worldwide. Americans eat about sixty pounds of beef per person per year, Argentines eat over twice that amount, while European consumption ranges widely from twenty to sixty-five pounds per year (10)(11). This is significant because well over one-third of the world's grain harvest is fed to livestock, including over 70% of the grain harvested in the United States (12). In addition, approximately 40% of deforestation can be attributed to clearing land for cattle grazing or for growing soybeans which will be fed to cattle (13).

Enough grain is produced globally to provide each human with 3,500 calories per day (14). Yet when grain calories are eaten and converted into beef, the total calories available to human consumption declines by 90% (15). That is, if a cow requires one million calories of grain to achieve its full weight, its meat only provides 100,000 calories of nutrition. That is salient when one considers how many people are starving on the planet. On the flip side of that equation is the fact that beef consumption is directly linked to the two biggest killers in the Western world – cancer and heart disease

Nice Point !

(atherosclerosis). When will we collectively see the writing on the wall and decide to change? Beef consumption is destroying our forests, depleting food surpluses, and diseasing and killing our bodies. Westerners don't need to be vegetarians; all that is necessary is that we *temper* our consumption of meat in the awareness of how much good it will do the planet and our bodies. Vandana Shiva, author of *Stolen Harvest*, points to the specific role of fast-food chains in this scenario:

"Junk-food chains, including KFC and Pizza Hut, are under attack from major environmental groups in the United States and other developed countries because of their environmental impact. Intensive breeding of livestock and poultry for such restaurants leads to deforestation, land degradation, and contamination of water sources and other natural resources. For every pound of red meat, poultry, eggs, and milk produced, farm fields lose about five pounds of irreplaceable top soil. The water necessary for meat breeding comes to about 190 gallons per animal per day, or ten times what a normal Indian family is supposed to use in one day, if it gets water at all" (16).

Beef production is indeed very water-intensive and fossil fuel-intensive because of the agri-business process that is required to produce the copious grain necessary to raise one beef cow. One gallon of gasoline is used to produce each pound of grain-fed beef, and half of all water consumed in the U.S. is used to grow grain for cattle feed (17).

The prescient management of water is indeed of highest priority in the 21st century natural resource equation. As stated in this book's introduction, the average U.S. household uses 145 gallons of water per day, while the averages in Spain and Ethiopia are 75 gallons and 5 gallons per day, respectively (18). In many industrialized societies, an illusion is cultivated of an unlimited supply of resources. The amount of water on Earth, though infinitely recyclable, is precisely finite. Over 97% of the water on Earth is salty ocean water, leaving 2.5% as fresh water. About 70% of this small amount of fresh water is frozen in mountain glaciers and the continental ice fields of Greenland and Antarctica. Of the tiny amount left, most fresh water is contained in deep underground aquifers (groundwater) or soil moisture. Therefore, the only water that we can regularly and easily access for our survival is from rain that falls and glaciers that melt, both flowing into lakes and rivers.

We all rely on this so-called hydrologic cycle to bring water to us. Water evaporates off of oceans and lakes, forms clouds, and falls as rain or snow. What is not taken up by plants percolates through soil and eventually into rivers and groundwater. Rivers run into the sea and the process begins again. The problem is, we are extracting water from rivers and groundwater faster than the Earth's hydrologic cycle can replenish them. Indeed, several rivers no longer reach the sea, including the formerly mighty Colorado River which once carved the Grand Canyon. The Aral Sea, previously the fourth-largest lake on the planet, is now totally gone due to water extraction for irrigation by regional farmers. Also, global warming is dramatically accelerating glacial melting, thereby depleting an important and steady source of fresh water.

Many desert communities get as much as 60% of their fresh water supply from groundwater, especially in drought years. Las Vegas, Nevada and Palm Springs, California are among them (19). The California cities of Barstow, Banning, and Indio glean 100% of their fresh water from groundwater reserves (20). If too much water is withdrawn at rates faster than the natural "recharge rate," then huge land subsidences can occur where giant sections of land simply sink several feet. This happened in California's San Joaquin Valley in 1977 because farmers were withdrawing over 48 billion gallons (150,000 acre feet) of water per day (21). In that year, literally one-half of this gigantic valley (5,200 square miles) sunk approximately one foot (22). Several small sections sank over fifteen feet. If we keep tapping these sources, desert plant roots can no longer reach the water table during drought, and pumping deeper and deeper becomes exorbitantly expensive, so massive desert communities will have to be abandoned.

When we over-allocate river water and continually increase the amount siphoned off, it has a huge effect on fish and aquatic populations, which of course we rely on for food. Only 40% of the original river water flow from the Sierra Nevada Mountains now reaches the San Francisco Bay. Its waters are tapped by cities as far away as Los Angeles, 400 miles to the south.

Some easy ways to save water are to install low-flow shower heads, take shorter showers, and the tried-and-true method of placing a brick in the toilet reservoir. Huge savings in water can be made by replacing a lawn with vegetation that requires little water such as succulent plants, ivy, or low shrubs. Even eating organic foods is an indirect way of saving water, since 87% of all fresh water used on Earth is put toward agricultural irrigation, and conventional agriculture requires more water than organic agriculture (23).

Faced with national water shortages, the current president of Brazil, Luiz da Silva, urged his citizens to urinate in the shower, saving millions of toilet flushes per day. Up to one-fourth of the world's countries' water resources are already stressed, and this is predicted to be dramatically exacerbated by the huge rise in population in coming decades. The World Health Organization estimates that five million people die each year from ingesting contaminated or heavily polluted water. By and large, this is not because they unknowingly ingest unhealthy water, but because they have no other choice but to drink contaminated water. Millions of developing world residents who have the means are forced to pay private distributors handsomely to acquire clean water, often up to one-third of their income.

Water management, conservation, and recycling are causes that call for championing by local and state governments. The fact that the water allotment for a single-family home in Southern California, a region that receives only about ten inches of rain per year, is 10,000 gallons per month offers a testament to the environmental escapism that many cities espouse (24). "Thirst" is a film that documents the growing global water crisis.

A worthy side note is how water and energy are intimately tied together. It requires water to make energy and it requires energy to transport water. Hundreds of gallons of water are used in coal-fired and nuclear energy production facilities to produce each megawatt hour of electricity, and a significant portion of the energy used in the American southwest is devoted simply to pumping and transporting water to urban destinations (25). It is important to state that solar energy production and wind energy production require little to no water, by comparison.

Gasoline is another substance whose consumption calls for wise stewardship, both because it is running out and due to its very harmful side effects. Americans consume more gasoline by far than any other nation. In my opinion, this is due to the fact that we are addicted to two things: horsepower and large vehicles. Our horsepower fixation is cultivated by advertisements that attempt to connect one's car's power to one's personal power. Highlighting the moment when you might explode down an empty woodland highway, these advertisements forget to mention that the other 99% of your driving time, that excessive and unnecessary horsepower will simply be guzzling gas as you slowly navigate urban traffic.

The notion that we all need a 300-horsepower sportscar in order to express and exert our dominance and uniqueness is both silly and irresponsible. More deceptive is the perceived need for ultra-powerful work trucks. The overwhelming majority of trucks and SUVs sold never haul heavy equipment or go off-roading, as depicted in commercials. Yet these monstrous vehicles are usually fully equipped to do so. The proud owner of a 2010 Ram 1500 truck can roar down the street to go pick up bread at the market with the "security" and power of 400 horses under the hood. The 2002 model of the same truck had only 245 horsepower.

This insidious escalation of horsepower gradually gets the public accustomed to inflated horsepower numbers, not to mention giant-sized trucks and SUVs, so that anything less seems insufficient. All the while, we are guzzling more and more gas since horsepower and car weight are usually inversely related to gas mileage. In other words, the more horsepower and the larger the vehicle, the poorer the gas mileage will be. Wider tires also lower gas mileage. Just for some perspective, Henry Ford's original Model T was equipped with a four-cylinder, twenty-horsepower engine, and the 1966 Volkswagen Beetle had only forty horsepower. These are two of the best-selling cars of all time and they were quite capable of moving people from point A to point B.

For the true speed lover and car enthusiast, there is actually one positive loophole where performance and sustainability come together: electric cars. Contrary to popular perception, electric-car motors are faster than gasoline-powered ones. Because power is generated by the repulsion of positive and negative electrical forces, electric motors give cars astonishingly high torque, resulting in exceptional zero to sixty times. One all-electric car on the market right now is the Tesla roadster. It gets over 200 miles to one charge, goes zero to sixty in 3.7 seconds, and produces no emissions. I recently rode in one and I can attest to the rocket-like acceleration. Most electric motors placed into hybrid cars are very down-sized and hence do not exhibit such impressive power. When they finally get a foothold in the market, electric cars will comprise a revolution in eco-friendly, high-performance, chic transportation.

Heavy suppression and outright sabotage of technology has precluded electric cars from entering the car market in earnest for over a century. This superior, powerful, and clean technology has been around for much longer than most of us are aware. In fact, there were more electric cars on U.S. roads in the year 1900 than gasoline-powered cars (26). Oil companies saw this as a threat and so they have consistently and very stealthily squelched every attempt at resurgence that the no-emissions auto industry has made. A recent such action was Texaco's buyout of Stan Oshinsky's patented battery technology in the mid 1990s, which was to be used in General Motors' EV-1 all-electric cars (27).

GM, together with an oil company coalition, also sued the state of California in 2001 when it attempted to mandate that 10% of all cars produced by auto manufacturers be totally emission-free. GM won the suit, despite the fact that a majority of Californians supported the mandate (28).

More egregious than that was a development that began with a seemingly innocuous portion of the 1997 U. S. tax code (section 179), which granted small business owners a $25,000 tax break for the purchase of a vehicle weighing over 6,000 pounds (29). Only the largest SUVs with the lowest fuel economy qualified for the cut. Yet in 2003, as a result of the Bush administration's efforts, that deduction was raised to a surprising $100,000. Addressing US energy secretary Spencer Abraham in an October 12, 2003 interview, *60 Minutes* reporter Lesley Stahl stated "…there's an encouragement for the small business person not just to stay afloat but to go buy the biggest gas guzzler there is… the 6,000 pound car… the biggest. Does that make sense? You can almost buy the whole car for the tax break." Soon after, the age of the SUV began in earnest in the U.S. and giant vehicles suddenly and conspicuously began to show up on our roads.

A year earlier, the IRS declared hybrid cars eligible for tax deductions, as well, under the Energy Policy Act of 1992 (PL 103-486). The maximum deduction was a mere $4,000 (30). Unless a citizen were uncommonly inquisitive into the written tax code, she would not unearth this garish incentive for Americans to turn away from environmentally friendly automobiles to the most offensive gas guzzlers available.

Whatever dismissive thought that pops into the head of the average U.S. citizen when he hears a discussion of electric cars is most likely the result of carefully calculated suppression, omission, or falsification of information about these wonderful cars. As in the case of the Tesla mentioned above, electric cars are fast, they have plenty of range, and they are virtually silent. But their two greatest virtues which place them head-and-shoulders above gasoline-powered cars is that electric cars, of course, produce no emissions, and they are essentially maintenance free. Electric motors have only one moving part and do not require oil for lubrication, water for cooling, nor air intake for combustion. There are no fuel pumps, valves, or alternators which are common causes of breakdowns. Even transmissions are significantly streamlined in electric cars and hence have fewer problems than conventional ones. Electric cars should have revolutionized urban transportation over a hundred years ago, and if they are allowed to, they will do nothing less than that today. Imagine our cities with dramatically less freeway or street noise, and no smog! That reality is quite attainable if we only know that it is possible and choose it.

I think, perhaps, that I always see possibility for new realities because in my travels, I witnessed such diverse approaches to life and so many valid philosophies about how to live it. This allowed me to look at my own culture with a more objective eye. One very effective way to surmise the lifestyle habits of a culture, though it may sound strange, is to examine their trash. In Thailand, I once rented a scooter and followed a garbage truck around all day in order to gain better insight into the volume and the nature of local consumption. A few years earlier in downtown Buenos Aires, I had seen homeless mothers and their children eating their nightly meal of leftover hamburger patties thrown into the dumpster behind a McDonald's restaurant.

Another occasion in Nairobi, Kenya, where I witnessed an unexpected fate for refuse, is worth a more detailed description. Sitting in a lot behind a small restaurant and eating my lunch of rice and curry, I saw a truck filled with trash pull up and promptly dump its contents into a fifty- by-fifty-foot space. Immediately, a few people peeked out from between the buildings and grabbed items from the pile that were salvageable – bike tires, a chair, a few dishes and a plate. After this, a second wave of curious pile-pickers identified and reclaimed usable materials such as string, swaths of leather, and any sizeable pieces of plastic or metal. Almost as if on cue, as the last few people left, four or five emaciated dogs crept in and gobbled up most of the uneaten food in the shrinking heap of garbage. The entire procession lasted the better part of an hour, finished off by a small flock of birds that descended on the pile and ate any remaining food. Only perhaps one-third of the original pile of trash now remained. I surmised that this sequence probably played out in exactly the same way every day. The relative poverty of the Nairobi region, no doubt, was the main incentive for such extensive reusing and recycling, but whatever the cause, such thorough and conscientious management of resources was a refreshing sight.

In stark contrast to this method of managing refuse, residents of the United States produce about 1.5 billion pounds of trash every day, and 500 billion pounds of trash per year (31). Thirty years ago, we produced half of that amount. Approximately 65% of this refuse is simply piled up in landfills, so our landfills are filling up, while new sites for dumps are increasingly difficult to locate (32). Capitalist economies like that in the United States are based on ever-increasing production and consumption. Because of this, our populace is kept largely unaware of the effects of our consumption on the environment, including fossil-fuel burning and trash production. Yet the ramifications of our habits are increasingly hard to ignore. Author Dorothy L. Sayers said in 1942 that "A society in which consumption has to be artificially stimulated in order to keep production going is a society founded on trash and waste, and such a society is a house built upon sand" (33). This imminent crisis is turning many heads toward the option of recycling.

Approximately 95% of all refuse produced is reusable or recyclable, while in the U.S. only 35% of the total garbage collected, the waste stream, is currently diverted from landfills to more environmentally-feasible destinations (34). Paper and food constitute over half of the contents of trash in America. Yard trimmings contribute another 10% approximately, while glass, metals, and plastics comprise 25%. Initial recycling efforts have focused on collecting and recycling paper, glass, aluminum, and plastics resulting in the fact that approximately 30% of the waste stream is currently recycled in the U.S. Globally, countries such as Germany and the Netherlands recycle close to two-thirds of their trash, while small nations such as Denmark, Japan, and Luxembourg are forced to burn over half of their trash due to space constraints.

When I pass a garbage truck or city dump, I don't see waste, I see energy, cash, fertilizer, and countless still useable items. This is what is in our trash, if we just take it to the right destination and allow them to convert it into these very desirable end products. In my San Fernando Valley neighborhood in Los Angeles, a man named "Buck" understands this. He used to be a boxer until he found that he made more money and could support his kids just by recycling full-time. He drives his truck up to all of the public dumpsters in the city and simply pulls out valuable recyclables. Though not a very glamorous job, he told me that he makes between forty and sixty thousand dollars per year! So for Buck, the trash is full of cash.

Trash is also full of valuable energy. For instance,

organic materials comprise about a third of all Municipal Solid Waste (MSW) in the U.S. today. That totals about forty million tons of yard trimmings and sixteen million tons of food that is thrown away each year. It was discovered that in landfills these materials generate methane gas which is harmful to the ozone layer, and toxic leachate that invades and pollutes local groundwater. One simple solution has been to separate food from the waste stream and burn the methane gas that it generates for heat energy. The conversion is termed "biomass utilization." Six Rwandan prisons with a population of 5,000 inmates each have implemented a similar process in which methane gas is siphoned off of toilet sewage and used to provide cooking fuel for the massive prison kitchens (35). This program has been successfully operated since 2001 and halves the amount of fuel wood that was formerly used in the prison system.

Energy that is found in trash or sewage cuts down on the amount of oil that must be fought for in the Middle East, or coal that must be dug up, transported, and burned. Waste to Energy (WTE) is another great method of gleaning energy from the waste stream, wherein the heat that is produced from burning dry solid waste is transformed into electricity. Gauged on emissions produced per each unit of electricity generated, WTE produces fewer emissions than coal plants and equal or less than natural gas plants (36).

Tokyo Waterfront Recycle Power Company is making money from trash while helping the environment. The company trucks waste to its site, recycles what it can, then burns what it cannot and converts the heat into enough electricity to power 55,000 homes in the area. It also filters the emissions from the burning for excess toxins (37). Following suit is one of Tokyo's largest commercial real estate developers, Mori Building Company. Green space, rainwater recycling, waste-heat recapture, and collective recycling plans are now standard in their housing developments (38).

Only two percent of Americans are farmers, so few of us realize how important and expensive fertilizer is. The massive tonnage of food and biodegradable materials thrown away each year in the waste streams of wealthy nations essentially amounts to piles of free fertilizer. The transformation into fertilizer is made possible by composting in which organic waste (food and yard trimmings) is allowed to biodegrade in a hot, moist environment for a few weeks. The product is high-quality, extremely valuable fertilizer. Many cities, including Los Angeles and San Francisco, compost residential yard waste, and the fertilizer product is then sold to local farmers. When I worked at *Raw Energy* organic café in Berkeley, California, my friend named Wendell, who was homeless, came by each day to pick up the bag of cellulose pulp that we had collected from our juicer. He took it to the Berkeley community organic garden where the cellulose was applied directly to the soil as organic compost fertilizer. Worms are even sometimes used in "vermi-composting" facilities in order to transform the waste into fertilizer within twenty-four hours!

Some food can be salvaged before it reaches the landfill. Many institutions such as churches, the Salvation Army, or other nongovernmental organizations have a long tradition of collecting and re-distributing excess food, such as canned goods, before it is thrown away. Today, these efforts have expanded due to companies like Feeding America, which is a network of 200 food banks across the country that passed out one billion pounds of food as far back as 2001 (39). These programs are invaluable, since in the 90s in California alone, 1.3 million residents went hungry, yet about four million tons of food is thrown away in the state every year (40).

One company called "Last Chance Mercantile" in Monterey, California truly brings to life the adage that one man's trash is another man's treasure. The company grosses over $200,000 per year by selling items recovered from the trash such as furniture, housewares, bicycles, and toys. A similar, yet larger, program in Berkeley called "Urban Ore" currently takes in well over one million dollars annually (41).

By reducing how much waste we create and recycling the trash that we do generate, we produce positive effects on both ends of the production line. First, fewer virgin materials need to be extracted from nature, such as trees for paper, bauxite ore for aluminum, or silica and lime for glass. This saves energy, creates less CO_2, and also takes less from the environment. For example, making a new aluminum can from a recycled can requires 95% less energy than making a can from raw materials. Second, less trash ends up at the dump. This saves money and CO_2 because fewer trucks have to transport the U.S.'s 1.5 billion pounds of trash per day, and it also reduces the air and water pollution that landfills produce. So rather than digging up so many raw materials, making new products, then throwing them away, we can simply re-use and recycle the products and materials that we already possess.

Many Native American tribes, the first inhabitants of North America, provided an excellent example of how to live in harmony with nature by taking only what they needed from nature and using all that they took. Every part of the buffalo was used, from the fur and the meat to the sinew and tendons. That shows a respect for and understanding of the environment. We have much larger populations to support today, so that kind of idealistic synergy may not be as plausible, yet simple awareness and a conscientious effort to waste less and reuse more would make significant changes. We can also learn from nature itself, where all minerals, organic materials, water and air on Earth have been recycled over and over for billions of years. The waste of one process – humans breathing in oxygen and exhaling carbon dioxide – becomes the building blocks of another process – plants taking in carbon dioxide and giving off oxygen. The same recycling process is evident in the cosmos with the life cycle of stars and galaxies.

I have always seen it as part of a divine design that the two most abundant elements in the Earth's terrestrial crust are silicon and aluminum. Because of this, geographers actually call the continental crust "Si-al." This is significant because silica (derived from silicon) is the main ingredient in glass, and glass and aluminum happen to be infinitely recyclable substances. They never lose their structural integrity, as opposed to paper or plastic, which can only be recycled a handful of times. It is as if these materials were placed right at our feet so we would assuredly use them and benefit from their sustainable utility.

Living more efficiently overall allows the industrialized world to shift from a disposable lifestyle to a sustainable lifestyle. Especially in the wealthy Western world, tempering our consumption of food, energy, and water, and lessening our production of waste is at the crux of this shift.

Industrialized economies have long been based on consumption, and therefore necessarily, upon waste. Awareness of notions such as landfill proliferation, the negative effects of eating processed foods, and global warming caused by CO_2 production might temper buying and consuming habits. Therefore, this tempered awareness is not promoted and even actively suppressed. Yet if politicians and business people can continue their efforts to step beyond assuaging certain powerful groups and struggling to keep day-to-day economic indicators favorable, they can help us all take a broader, more responsible view of our economy, our precious health, and our irreplaceable resources (42). This touches upon another necessary belief shift: changing our definition of wealth from money to our personal health, the health of the planet, and those we love. The health of our bodies, planet, and loving relationships are real and perennial. They form the regenerative source of our future.

If efficient household habits such as recycling, water and energy conservation, and healthy eating were supported, promoted, and subsidized by governments of wealthy nations where these practices are most needed, they would undoubtedly flourish. This is already occurring on a large scale in a few European nations such as Germany and Denmark.

On the contrary, the oil and agribusiness industries have long been strongly affiliated with and/or heavily subsidized by the U.S. federal government. This affords these industries great success and productivity. Yet how would they fare without such massive help and partnership with the government? Said industries have decades of proven environmental damage on their scorecard, yet they are staffed with intelligent, highly capable people who I see as critical components in generating solutions to the world's pressing biological and technological challenges. I invite these individuals to be a welcomed and necessary part of the planet's transformation. Influence from the more progressive current U.S. governmental administration may help to precipitate such change.

A departure from the predominantly economic, localized, and short-term basis for our decisions about food, energy, water, and refuse is now called for. This will help to promote a wholehearted embracing of policies and lifestyle habits that are holistic and sustainable long into the future. This is wise husbandry of our resources. This is conscious foresight. Many countries in the developing world have always operated in this way. It is ever more important that citizens and leaders in the developed world continue to expand their commendable efforts to join in this trend.

The Gift of Tragedy

Visions of a Bold and Inevitable Future for the United States and the World

"History is a race between education and catastrophe."

- H.G. Wells

Today on this Earth, 15,000 people will starve to death. Thousands of girls will be forced into the sex trade, 100,000 acres of rainforest will be cut down, and a few hundred thousand members of the U.S. military will arise and patrol a foreign country.

Most of us in the Western world have a vague understanding of these realities, but it is often very easy for us to continue life as usual – picking out tile for the new bathroom, rounding our triceps at the gym, watching our favorite reality TV show – all while others beseech the heavens for a bag of rice or a life-saving penicillin shot for their child.

And so sometimes we need a wake-up call to return our focus to what is essential in this life and on this Earth. We've been getting them frequently of late:

9/11
The Tsunami in Asia
Hurricane Katrina
The 2009 global financial crisis
The 2010 Haiti and Chile earthquakes
The Icelandic Volcano ceasing European air traffic
The BP oil geyser in the Gulf of Mexico

These huge and jarring events come along and they
shake us to our core – for the very purpose of reminding
us *of* our core – those we love, our health, and the health
of our home, this planet. The messages of 9/11 and of the
tsunami, while apparent immediately, are even more clear in
retrospect. 9/11 evoked the greatest show of national unity
and compassion for fellow Americans that most of us have
ever witnessed. It also had the potential to grant us a new
perspective on the implications of our government's activities
in the Middle East, which many agree are related to this
tragedy. But this realization, en masse, was not actualized.
The tsunami, because its victims were locals as well as tourists
from all over the world, had the amazing effect of creating
an instant global consciousness. All of us were hurt, all of us
were affected, all of us were helping. It was an astonishing
equalizer and it provided an effective experience of our
interconnectedness. It also served to bring an outpouring of
help, resources, and Western attention onto some of the most
destitute parts of the world – namely, Indonesia and India.

In a larger sense, and perhaps in some benefit to the
world, the Haiti earthquake of 2010 jarred us enough to cut
through our cultural myopia and daily routines and let us see
how bad conditions really are, even so close to a wealthy nation
like the U.S. Surprising to many who watched the devastation
on television was that even before the quake, Haiti was in dire
straits and was the poorest country in the western hemisphere.
We were all implored to sit and gaze upon the despair of our

close island neighbors, and millions were spurred to offer help in one form or another.

Natural and human-induced disasters are an effective way for the living Earth and the collective human consciousness to communicate with us as individuals. The Earth is a dynamic living system which displays an amazing ability to adapt and rebalance itself after destabilizing events and eras on the globe. In this way the Earth could be said to be one whole living organism, or even to have a consciousness. Perhaps the recent substantial and documented rise in the frequency of natural disasters is the Earth's way of rebalancing itself and of waking us up so that we may come into harmony with it. Human-induced disasters like 9/11 could be said to arise in a similar way, in that an unacknowledged part of society, or the collective human consciousness, has asserted itself so that we must take notice and begin to come into harmony with *it*. One Saudi terrorist leader said "If our messages had been able to reach you through words, we wouldn't have been delivering them through planes" (1). Jarring events, both human and environmental in source, arise to bring awareness to parts of humanity which are isolated or which do not perceive themselves or their actions to be affecting the larger whole.

Hurricane Katrina jarred and affected many of us, but have we gotten the insights that it has sent us? The shock has passed but have we still not yet imbibed the inherent messages that the hurricane has provided? If any jarring event comes into our life and our response is only sadness or shock or anger or confusion, then we have not received the message, and another wake-up call is likely to come. She did. Her name, this time, was Hurricane Rita, but the message was still the same. And so, we must look to the deeper messages that Katrina and Rita offer to us. Because the only reason any "tragedy" arises is so that a greater ongoing tragedy can be brought to our attention, and stopped.

The first result and message that Katrina provided was to bring our government's focus back onto home turf. Our government, for good or bad, often spends a large portion of its energies, money and focus on endeavors outside of this country. Fighting wars, acquiring new markets and resources for our mega-corporations, and involving ourselves in the affairs of various nations across the globe leaves less time to focus on our own people, our own cities, our own issues. Katrina reminded us of that. Also due to Katrina, many in this country have acquired a true sympathy for those in other nations who are in catastrophic, desperate situations. It is often very easy for us to get lost in our lives of entertainment and relative luxury and to passively ignore the obvious tribulations of much of the rest of the world. The hurricane gave us a visceral first-hand feeling of commonality with the struggles in the developing world, in particular the millions of dislocated peoples and refugees that we see depicted on television so often. One New Orleans woman said it best when viewing images of her city in shambles, "It looks like the third world."

An additional, though perhaps less major, message from Katrina was to display that in any and all situations, from coups d'état to hurricanes to bake sales, our government has often had one unilateral response: military presence. It appeared inappropriate in a scene of such tragedy, death, and despair, to inject heavily-armed national guardsmen to walk the streets with orders to shoot anyone trying to loot food or basic survival supplies. I do understand that chaos needed to be subdued; I heard countless first-hand accounts from close friends living in New Orleans. Yet it seems that amidst such a tragedy the more fitting response would be to focus on providing overflowing empathy and care.

Another human-induced "disaster," the global financial crisis of 2009, seems to have gotten virtually everyone's attention. For a brief moment we saw into the dicey innards of lending institutions and stock markets and how they sometimes recklessly manage or even take other people's money. I admired the presidents and members of congress of various countries who pushed for circumspection and caution when delivering bail-out money to their domestic institutions. In the U.S., the financial crisis uncovered significant corruption and mismanagement and, thankfully, generated more oversight and supervision of these oligarchic big-money players.

I had a wake-up call of my own several years ago while on a flight over central Bolivia. One of the plane's engines failed and we immediately began to plummet toward the Earth. Losing cabin pressure, the oxygen masks dropped down and histrionics ensued. Amidst this total chaos, images of my family back home in California came into my head and I could think about nothing else. I felt utterly alone – crash landing in a plane in Bolivia, seated next to complete strangers – but I was shown in that moment what, and who, was truly important to me. The pilot eventually regained control and made a successful emergency landing.

One-time precipitous events like hurricanes and crash landings often serve as excellent wake-up calls, but on an everyday basis globally, there are ongoing crises that also demand our attention. These are the broad categories of struggle which have been outlined in this book: sex and labor trades, rampant starvation, rapid climate change, and war over energy and resources. Hopefully this list of global ills will make us pause and ask "What's going on in the world today that produces such suffering, imbalance, and separation?"

The response to this question evokes a list of the usual suspects: the source can be pinpointed to attitudes of fear and greed in the West inciting subjugation of the world's poorer economies, along with a myopic over-consumption and lack of global awareness. This is linked to a palpable desperation and struggle to survive in the third world, resulting in the sale of human beings and of nature itself. This mix of fear, greed, myopia, and desperation is propagating AIDS through a thriving sex trade, malnutrition through widespread starvation, and even malaria, through the simple lack of enough mosquito nets. Greed and myopia have also allowed high levels of fossil fuel pollution and deforestation to generate climate change and the rapid loss of biodiversity through species extinction. Not fully acknowledging these unhealthy attitudes and actions is perpetuating the ensuing corporal and terrestrial diseases that are sourced in them – malnutrition, AIDS, pollution, and global warming. These are fundamental realities of our globe today which we may deliberately make ourselves aware of, rather than waiting for a "wake-up call" from nature or society.

But why do we continue to need such jarring wake-up calls in recent months and years? Specifically, why do we, here in America, need to be awakened? The answer is, simply, that we live in isolation and distraction. We are isolated from the world's problems physically, by two oceans, and ideologically, by the carefully-selected media images that give us a limited view of the world outside of our cultural bubble. At the same time, there is such a deluge of these selected images and information that our innate desire to investigate the world around us is effectively overwhelmed and we are goaded to return to the local, more manageable level. Approximately 20% of Americans own a passport, while that number is tripled in most European countries. Moreover, the average European or African speaks two to three languages, but most Americans, especially non-recent immigrants, speak only English.

The modern Western denizen has days filled with sound and fury: coffee fixes, errands to run, tweets to read and send, and yet sometimes devoid of global awareness and deeper significance. I believe that America and its citizens, having amply achieved subsistence individually, and unmatched global influence nationally, long for a new goal.

Our hearts ache in the deep subconscious awareness that there are so many problems on this Earth, so many of us suffering, and yet many of us do very little about it. This lack of purpose may literally be killing us. Without a purpose, a cause, a goal that animates us and in some way affects the world, our hearts are literally in dis-ease. We in the U.S. and the West are aching to be, to help, to strive, to ameliorate, to express our power – but that magnanimous, active being is not fully expressed. We are a racehorse locked in its stable, a muscle car with no road on which to roar. And each day that this goes on, our soul, the heart of who we are, dies a small death. And so in this developed world, the number one killer is disease of the heart or heart disease: the symptom of an unengaged self, an unexpressed soul.

Some of this need is indeed finding expression in the form of magnanimous individuals and organizations which are offering help where it is most needed. The environmental movement, the push for universal human rights, and rapid disaster relief responses are evidence of this philanthropy. Countless careers burgeon in the green economy and in the holistic sectors of business, health care, and the food industry. Yet the activities of perhaps the majority of Westerners still do not extend beyond their own microcosm, and they are often not connected to a larger social cause.

In order to fill the void left by a lack of purpose on a societal level, the assortment and accessibility of entertainment must grow. Each day our minds and bodies are flooded with entertainment and stimulation: from countless cable-television channels and an entire apothecary of recreational drugs to 5,000-song iPods, elaborate video games for adults, and phones that connect us in real-time to the daily events of hundreds of other people. That is not to mention countless other services and images aimed at corporal and mental stimulation. This deluge can effectively nudge our attention off of any substantive national or global-level concerns. Our soul ravenously pursues expression and fulfillment, yet in the absence of true self-expression and without conscientious guidance it will accept whatever shows up.

Therefore, wake-up calls may also arise in order to pull us away from our copious distractions. One principal mode of distraction in American society is fear, the main source of which over the past decade are entities that stoke our fear of terrorist attack. Rather than urging us to look into what caused 9/11, we are taught to simply fear further attacks or to fear Muslims. When human beings experience acute fear of an external threat, our primal "fight-or-flight" response is engaged, and we become totally focused on averting immediate danger. This response to a potential threat is natural, yet when this primal response is continually activated day after day, our attention is never allowed to settle on rational daily or domestic issues. Constant and acute fear also goads us into relinquishing many of our freedoms in the name of safety.

Consumerism is also an omnipresent distraction from living out our purpose. This is true in many western cultures, including Europe, North America, Japan, Australia, New Zealand, and increasingly, China. The idea that we must constantly consume all manner of substances, experiences, objects and even ideas in order to simply get through each day is a central tenet of life in many developed nations. Television, consumerism's greatest tool, shifts our brains from an active and alert state of Beta-wave production to a much slower Alpha-wave state, clinically similar to a light hypnosis. Consistent television viewers shift to this passive, suggestible Alpha state often within a minute of turning on the tube (2). Commercials manufacture demand by hawking their wares directly into our undefended brains. Due to marketing, packaging, and advertising, a homogenization of products is created whereby the conditions, laborers, and natural materials which came together to produce an item are very effectively obscured. This keeps Western consumers insulated from an awareness of how their purchases might be perpetuating harmful global trends. The simple act of constantly buying and consuming is a ubiquitous and powerful distraction in our society and it can keep us centered on our individual needs, and on the local bounded scale.

Hence, broadly, through fear, consumerism, and entertainment developed world denizens are kept distracted, numbed, over-stimulated, and yet still under-engaged. In the absence of a real goal, our desire still spills forth, and it emerges in myriad ways: stress from an imbalanced focus on money and career, diseased hearts from a lack of true connection and purpose in the world, and excess weight from sedentary lives. These are our national diseases, the symptoms of our lack of actualized agency, the evidence of our stalled, aching, imploding potential.

That said, in the West, a marked productivity has nonetheless occurred which has generated prosperity over the last few centuries and pushed the world forward. Technological and industrial innovation, ingenuity, and human capital the world over allows for constant evolution and re-creation of national economies. Aviation has given way to space exploration, doctors now treat our bodies on the microbial level, and friendship groups can now be electronic rather than physical. Societal progress, too, is moving into a new realm. The next step for the world's wealthy nations is shifting from individual goals to collective ones and seeking progress through collaboration, rather than through competition. In a word, this depicts a state of compassion.

Humanity is always pushing to do more, to be more, and to move forward. We now yearn for a larger, collective mission through which to focus our tremendous energy and unequaled efficacy. That mission and focus, I believe, is international compassion and benevolence. Moving into a state of compassion will be the last power move for the wealthy nations, and the ultimate and sustainable strategy in international diplomacy. This ideological shift will represent the arrival of the final stage of development for the industrialized world.

Virtually every powerful western society has moved through an evolution which has been based on the acquisition of money and power – first colonialism then manufacturing then technology and then information and entertainment. Next and finally, because its own needs are sufficiently met, a society's goals can make the critical shift from an inward focus to an outward focus. Nascent expressions of benevolent societies are now observable in parts of Europe. Northern and Western Europe display the highest quality of life on the planet, and this region also contains some of the most compassionate and environmentally aware nations on Earth.

By the late 20th century the U.S. had already achieved a good measure of global dominance financially, culturally, and politically, but its oligarchic cravings for more markets and resources ravenously marched it forward. The terminus of this approach, however, is within sight, as evidenced by the casualties of its over-evolved hegemony: the deaths it causes in overseas wars, its bankrupted national purse, and the diminished quality – from lack of attention – of many domestic institutions, infrastructures, and amenities. The government's sluggish response to the devastation in New Orleans is a vivid example of this.

In the past 200 years, the evolution of America's goals and collective purpose has been as follows: Independence from England . . . Check. Manifest Destiny . . . . Check. Global hegemony . . . Check. Influencing the financial, political, and cultural current of the planet. . . .Check. Though on different timelines, much of the developed world has hit similar milestones. There is now a palpable yearning for that next stage, something new that goes beyond past hackneyed benchmarks.

Without a new collective goal, much of the Western world seems to have pushed into more distraction, more excess, and more risky and abusive economic endeavors. Enter the global financial meltdown of 2009. What we crave is a totally fresh, magnanimous direction in which to channel our considerable brain-power, resources and latent energy in the West.

At the same time, a huge portion of the Earth is destitute, struggling, and beleaguered. They suffer and scrape for survival in a fiercely competitive globe which leaves them consistently at the bottom. As we in the West gradually and sometimes poignantly wake up to our true purpose, and simultaneously to the troubling realities on this planet, we will see that our desire for purpose and the developing world's need for care, attention, and true problem-solving are perfect complements for each other. What will give us the greatest joy and satisfaction and expression of who we are is to use our ingenuity and considerable resources to ameliorate human struggle in the poorest sections of the globe. And this exact response from us is precisely what the developing world desires most – to be helped, supported, and acknowledged as equals, rather than subjugated, by the entities that have the power and the choice to do either one. Developing world leaders have a tall order themselves. They must work to expose corruption and eschew cultural isolation, both of which hamper international collaboration, and hence, development.

Evidence of a collaborative spirit was seen in President Obama's inauguration speech. In the following sentence, (which was likely in his own words because it does not appear in the official speech transcript) the new president conveyed a rather revolutionary sentiment:

"To all the other peoples and governments who are watching today . . . know that America is a friend of each nation, and every man, woman and child who seeks a future of peace and dignity – and we are ready to lead once more."

I believe that this is what we as individuals and nations want most – a true cause, a task which profoundly affects the world. In your hand, you have *5 Ways to Save the Planet*, and beyond these there are always more ways to help. A consistent dose of our help and attention would heal huge portions of what ills the most destitute parts of this globe on a scale that is perhaps unimaginable. The most refreshing new direction for us, in the Western nations, will be to give the world what we have always given to ourselves – opportunity, the power of self-determination, and in following, prosperity and abundance. And the most healing, gratifying experience for those in need would be to know, simply, that help is on the way.

And for the citizens and politicians who equate compassion with weakness and who still long for the traditional, more archaic expressions of power, what bigger power rush can there be than to be at the helm of a league of wealthy, altruistic nations and choose to usher the globe into an unprecedented level of egalitarian prosperity? We have this power in the U.S. and in all industrialized nations. And in every political and personal encounter, compassion is always the evidence of greatest power, while attack and avarice reek of desperation and weakness.

For good or bad, we as a nation in the U.S. have never let anything stand in our way. Americans have always been trend setters, innovators, and the hardest workers that I've ever witnessed. As an amalgam of immigrants from every country on Earth, we managed to build the globe's most powerful nation in less than 200 years. I am proud both of America's prodigious past and its imminent benevolent future.

Moreover, the truth of our country, the feeling and essence laid down by our forefathers – the belief in the equality of all human beings, and of the pursuit of health, happiness, and freedom – is still the foundation of who we are. It lives in the hearts of American citizens. We have always been a home for those fleeing oppression, a haven for those in need, a beacon of light for the world.

And now, at this critical turning point in history, the

collective political, cultural, and economic prowess and influence of the U.S. along with the Western countries reaches every corner of the globe. For this reason, the redirection of our national foci from individual goals to collective ones would constitute one of the greatest social and political shifts that the world has ever seen. At the same time, citizens and leaders of the developing world have the task of overcoming both corruption and isolation. A critical mass of people and nations are awakening and accepting the responsibility of bringing balance to global society.

As citizens and governments of developed nations, it is simply our choice in the coming years whether we will continue to consume without limit and support governmental and corporate aggression overseas, or if we will finally let go of the need for conquest, extend our hand to the most downtrodden nations, and commit to building a mutually abundant future...together.

Some Practical Suggestions for Taking Action on the 5 Ways to Save the Planet:

CONVERTING TO SOLAR:

If you own your home, several companies will now install solar panels for no money down and make your monthly payments to be less than your current electric bill. In other words, by going solar, you instantly SAVE money. Solar City – mentioned in this book – is a particularly large solar company which offers exceptional deals. It serves customers in Texas, California, Oregon, Colorado, and Arizona. Wherever you live, make sure to get estimates from multiple solar companies to ensure that you get the best deal available. Another frequent option is to take out a small loan to pay for the solar panels and installation. Then craft your loan payments so they are similar in size than your former electric bill payments. When the loan is paid, you have free electricity for decades! Moreover, solar-equipping a home usually increases its value.

Please always remember that if you don't own your home, you can still have a big impact by voting for solar and wind power to be implemented in your state. Critical renewable energy legislation is frequently up for voter approval and it cannot move forward without the enthusiastic support of concerned people like you and me. In fact, it is just as important to vote for and spread the word about renewables as it is to buy and invest in renewables. Coal and oil lobbies are big, powerful, and well-funded and they can skew and shade the appearance of landmark environmental legislation to make it seem like a bad idea to the average voter. Clean energy needs your assistance in the voting booth as much as anywhere. Many environmental groups and NGOs implement calling campaigns to get the word out on important legislation, and volunteering to be an earnestly concerned call operator is a giant help to them.

I should say that all renewable energy sources, including solar, wind, wave, geothermal, biomass, hydroelectric, and various biofuels, are superior alternatives to fossil fuels. They simply vary in applicability and relative environmental impact. I put such heavy emphasis on solar power, and to a lesser extent wind power, because I see them as the most viable options for broad worldwide adoption with the greatest ease and least environmental impact.

EATING ORGANIC:

The best places to find organic food are Whole Foods, Trader Joe's, Safeway, Albertson's and Harris Teeter Markets, or at your local farmer's market. In the U.S. east and south, Hannaford, Publix and Food Lion Markets also have large organic food sections.

Many organic farms are CSA – Community Supported Agriculture. These CSAs receive $20-$50 per month from hundreds of members. Members, in turn, receive a large box – usually twice a month – full of whatever fresh produce has ripened and been picked on the farm. You can usually find a CSA in your area with a quick internet search.

GIVING:

This simple idea is based on the fact that Europe, North America, Japan, Australia, and New Zealand are so wealthy compared to the developing world that giving even a small amount of money – to us – has a big and lasting impact on the poorest regions. To some extent, it matters less who or what you choose to support – the environment, women, disaster relief – and more that you just offer support of some kind to the entities in the world that are truly struggling.

If you are a young person or don't have money to give, as mentioned before, you can volunteer at call centers for your favorite organization and help to raise awareness or funds. Excellent opportunities to offer your physical labor or presence are available with Habitat for Humanity (www.habitat.org) which builds houses in the U.S. and in countless countries, and the Earth Corps (www.earthcorps.org) which offers a slew of pro-environment projects inside the U.S. On the local scale, community and city event calendars are riddled with clean-up days, tree plantings, food drives, and recycling days that would benefit from your energy, spirit, and helping hand.

There are innumerable avenues for volunteering internationally. Two of the most broadly based groups are Service Civil International of the International Volunteer Service (www.sci-ivs.org) and Global Volunteers (www.globalvolunteers.org).

Call your local chamber of commerce, city hall, or library to inquire about volunteering in your local area. There are so many ways to give, be it donating money, making calls to raise awareness, providing physical labor for a project, or just showing up and giving your love at a home for the elderly, an orphanage, or at a talk about a topic that you believe in.

When you give, you make connections and your own abundance expands. The feeling of purpose in your life grows, and you become more than you were.

UPLIFTING WOMEN:

The easiest way to help the most disadvantaged women – those in the developing world – is to donate money to non-profit organizations such as:

www.womenforwomen.org
www.globalfundforwomen.org
www.unicef.org
www. care.org
www. womankind.org.uk
www. amnesty.org
www. promujer.org (focusing on Latin America)
www. unifem.org

Simply becoming aware of the plight of disenfranchised and oppressed women across the globe is a very powerful act in itself. Understanding archaic gender-biased beliefs in your own country and the egregious gender inequalities in repressive societies is a key to initiating change.

A good way to start is by reading New York Times Pulitzer Prize-winning columnist Nicholas Kristof's book, *Half the Sky: Turning Oppression into Opportunity for Women Worldwide*.

MAKING YOUR HOUSEHOLD MORE EFFICIENT:

Recycle. If your neighborhood trash collectors or apartment building do not actively recycle, virtually every city has a recycling center, as do many Ralph's supermarkets. You can bring your recyclables to these locations and get paid for the paper, plastic, aluminum, and glass that you bring. As a very young child, I can remember my neighbor, Mrs. La Fornara, enlisting us to pile newspapers to the brim of her Volkswagen van. We would bring the paper to the nearby recycling center to collect $10 to $20, which seemed like a fortune at the time.

Save energy. One of the simplest, least expensive, and most immediate ways to save energy and CO_2 is by replacing your home's light bulbs with compact fluorescent lights, or CFLs (the ones that look like a swirly-tubed ice cream cone). They use about 80% less energy than regular light bulbs and usually last seven to ten YEARS. If each American household – 110 million in all – replaced one 60-watt bulb with a CFL, the energy saved would be equivalent to turning off two entire coal-fired energy plants (1). That's just from replacing one bulb. The average American home has over 50 bulb sockets. That amounts to astonishing potential energy savings from this one inexpensive, reliable, miraculous light bulb. Buying "Energy Star" brand appliances is also an easy way to save energy all day long, every day.

Using less gasoline is achievable by buying more hybrids, keeping your tires properly inflated, and even buying tires that are slightly less wide. The sudden preponderance of overly-wide "performance" tires has helped to dramatically reduce overall gas mileage of late in the United States. Even a small change in tire width will produce noticeable results. Try it!

Also, several companies currently produce all-electric zero emission cars that you can charge right at home, such as the Nissan Leaf ($30,000), the Tesla Roadster (0-60mph in 3.7 seconds), and the Th!nk City and Zenn Car, the latter two are available in Europe. Other companies like Reva and Mitsubishi produce electric cars for consumers in India and Asia, respectively. Countless models of electric cars are in development by Mercedes-Benz, BMW, Renault, Toyota, Nissan, Mini, and Chevrolet. As part of the U.S. economic stimulus bill of 2009, thirty electric car battery factories will soon be in operation, compared to two factories only a year ago.

For the no-holds-barred "go green" enthusiast, it is possible to convert any car to an all-electric car with less trouble than you might imagine. If you are mechanically-inclined, do-it-yourself conversion kits can be purchased online, parts included, for around $5,000. For about twice that amount many private garages will do the conversion for you. To access this sizeable network of technicians and businesses, the following websites are good resources:

> www.eaaev.org (Electric Automobile Association)
> www.panhandleev.org
> www.hybridcars.com/electric-car (the home-base for information on the subject)

Conserve water. Some water-saving tips are to shorten your showers by one or two minutes (saves 5 gallons per day), install low-flow shower heads (saves up to 20 gallons per day), only do full loads of dishes or laundry (saves 10-50 gallons per load of laundry), and fix leaky faucets (saves up to 20 gallons per day). These statistics are all taken from www.bewaterwise. com, which is a website dedicated to helping Southern California residents save water, but it is helpful to anyone who is interested in conserving water.

Also, plant vegetation in your yard that requires little, if any, irrigation, especially if you live in an arid region like the Southwestern U.S. Succulent plants, juniper bushes, shrubs, and non-broad leafed plants are good choices. Ask at your local nursery for good water-wise plant choices. If you do water your yard, do it before 8:00 am to reduce evaporation (saves 25 gallons per day). Use a broom instead of a hose to clean driveways and sidewalks (up to 150 gallons saved each time), and check your sprinkler system for leaks, overspray, and broken sprinkler heads (up to 500 gallons per month saved).

Remember that it requires enormous amounts of energy to transport water from the natural source to residences, and it consumes large quantities of water to produce energy in traditional power plants. So saving water and energy go hand in hand!

Be globally conscious as well as health conscious about what we eat. The foods that are best for your body are also best for the planet. Eat less food from a package, can, or box because these products tend to contain preservatives, artificial colorings, artificial sweeteners, and chemical flavor enhancers. Stick to food that's fresh and in its natural form. A guideline is that if a food or product wasn't available 500 years ago, then don't eat it. Another basic guideline is to shop the perimeter of the grocery store. This is where the fresh food is kept because the chillers that keep it cool need to be plugged into wall outlets. Food in the interior of markets usually has a shelf life of six months to two years!

Two things that Western denizens eat too much of are meat and sugar. Each day the average American consumes a half pound of meat and 20 teaspoons of refined sugar. We are so conditioned to these high levels of intake that some of us have come to believe that anything less would constitute an austere and incomplete diet. Quite the opposite is true. In fact, millions of people worldwide never eat sugar or meat, and rather than wasting away, they are almost invariably some of the healthiest people alive, and across myriad societies.

I do not suggest that we all become vegetarians, just that we cut down a bit on the amount and frequency of eating sugar and meat. After all, they lead to three of our biggest killers in the Western world: diabetes, atherosclerosis, and cancer.

I, myself, was 90% vegan for a few years, so I ate almost no meat or animal products. I never felt physically healthier, though I admit that being vegan definitely takes time and effort. My diet is still quite healthy, but now I eat some meat and/or dairy at least once a week. Moderation is key.

Citations and Bibliography

Introduction

1. Nisbett, R. 2003, *The Geography of Thought: How Asians and Westerners Think Differently...and Why.* Free Press, New York.
2. Geddes, R. and Lueck, D, 2002. "The Gains from Self-Ownership and the Expansion of Women's Rights." American Economic Review, American Economic Association. Vol. 92(4), pgs. 1079-1092, and World Population Data Sheet 2007.
3. UN Development Program – Human Development Report 2006. Accessed May, 2010 from: http://www.data360.org/dsg.aspx?Data_Set_Group_Id=757

Collective Global Awareness

1. Information Society Statistics. Data 1997-2002. European Commission, 2003.
2. Wilson, Michele A. 2006. *Technically Together: Rethinking Community within Techno-Society*. Peter Land: 6.
3. Crothers, L. 2007. *Globalization and American Popular Culture*. Rowman & Littlefield Publishers, Inc. Boulder, 60.
4. Crothers, 2007: 58.

5. Barber, Benjamin. 1995. *Jihad vs. McWorld: Terrorism's Challenge to Democracy*. Ballantine Books, New York.
6. Crothers, 2007.
7. Crothers, 2007: 62.
8. Crothers, 2007: 62.
9. Crothers, 2007: 140.
10. Chronological sequence taken from Gore, A. 2005, "An Inconvenient Truth" documentary film.

Other Sources

Barlow, "A Declaration of the Independence of Cyrberspace" Online: http://www.eff.org/pub/publications/john.perry. barlow/barlow.0296.declaration. Accessed May 2002.

Dyson, Ester, 1998. Release 2.1: *A Design for Living in the Digital Age.* London: Penguin Books.

Mattelart, Armand, 2003. *The Information Society: An Introduction.* Sage Publications.

Poster, Mark, 1995. *The Second Media Age.* Cambridge Polity Press: 24.

Preston, Paschal, 2001. *Reshaping Communications: Technology, Information and Social Change.* Sage Publications. London.

Ross, Gina, 2003. *Beyond the Trauma Vortex: The Media's Role in Healing Fear, Terror, and Violence.* North Atlantic Books. Berkeley.

Sky corporate 'factsheet,' http://media.corporate.ir.net/media_ files.Ise/bsy. UK/factsheet.pdf. Accessed June 1995.

Wired 1996, 'The Wired Manifesto.' October 1996: 42-7.

Damsel in Distress

1. Kingsolver, B. 2010. "Water is Life" *National Geographic*, April.
2. Douglas, B. 1997. "Global Sea Rise: A Redetermination," *Surveys in Geophysics*, (18) 2,3: May. Pgs. 279-292, and Church J. and White N. 2006. "A 20th Century Acceleration in Global Sea-Level Rise." *Geophysical Research Letters* (33).
3. Intergovernmental Panel on Climate Change (IPCC) report, 2007.
4. Clark, Robert P. 2000, *Global Life Systems: Population, food, and disease in the process of globalization.* Rowman & Littlefield, Oxford UK, pg 282, and Gore, A. 2005, documentary film "An Inconvenient Truth."
5. Antholis W. and Talbott S., 2010 "Leaving a Good Legacy: Why the ethical case for combating climate change is one that should appeal to conservatives." *Time magazine*, June 14, pg 24
6. Wald M., 2007, "Science Panel Disputes Estimates of US Coal Supply." *New York Times*, June   21.
7. U.S. Energy Information Administration: http://www.eia. doe.gov/fuelrenewable.html, Accessed July 2010.
8. www.guardian.co.uk/environment/datablog/2009dec/07/copenhagen-climate-change-summit, Accessed May 2010.
9. www.wikipedia.org/globalco2emissions, Accessed April 2010.
10. www.mongabay.com/0907.htm, and others, Accessed April 2010.
11. www.sciencemag.org, Accessed April 2010.
12. http://sd.defra.gov.uk/2010/03/fighting-the-scourge-of-illegal-logging-sustainable developtment-in-action/, Accessed May 2010.
13. Oster S. 2006, "Illegal Power Plants, Coal Mines in China Pose Challenge for Beijing." *The Wall Street Journal*, Dec. 27.

14. www.rainforests.mongabay.com/1024.htm, Accessed May 2010.
15. www.rainforests.mongabay.com/1024.htm, Accessed May 2010.
16. www.guardian.co.uk/environment/datablog/2009dec/07/ copenhagen-climate-change-summit, Accessed May 2010.
17. Antholis W. and Strobe T., 2010. "Leaving a Good Legacy: Why the ethical case for combating climate change is one that should appeal to conservatives." *Time Magazine,* June 14, pg. 24.

Myopia, Indulgence, and Desperation

1. Symington, A. 2005 "From Tragedy and Injustice to Rights and Empowerment: accountability in the economic realm" within Wilson, Shamillah, Anasuya Sengupta, and Kristy Evans, Eds., 2005. *Defending Our Dreams: Global feminist voices for a new generation.* Zed Books, London, pg. 40.

Human Traffic

1. Campagna, Daniel S., and Donald L. Poffenberger, 1988. *The Sexual Trafficking in Children: An Investigation of the Child Sex Trade.* Auburn House, Dover, Mass.
2. http://www.pbs.org/wgbh/pages/frontline/slaves/etc/stats. html, Accessed March 2006.
3. http://www.unescobkk.org/index.php?id=1022, Accessed March 2006.
4. U.S. Department of State, 2004. *Trafficking in Persons Report.* Washington, D.C.: U.S. Department of State.
5. UN estimates, found in State Department Trafficking in Persons Report, 2003.
6. ILO, A global alliance against forced labor: 2005.
7. Clawson, David L. and Merrill L. Johnson, 2003. *World*

Regional Geography: A development approach. Prentice Hall, 510.

8. "Owed Justice: Thai Women Trafficked into Debt Bondage in Japan," 2000. Human Rights Watch. New York, Washington.

9. ILO, A global alliance against forced labor: 2005.

10. "Owed Justice: Thai Women Trafficked into Debt Bondage in Japan," 2000: 6.

11. Skrobanek, Siriphon, Nattaya Bookpakdi, and Chutima Janthakeero, 1997. *The traffic in women: human realities of the international sex trade.* Zed Books. London.

12. Asia Migrant Bulletin. July-December, 1995. Volume III. No. 3&4.

13. Williams, Phil, Ed., 1999. *Illegal Immigration and Commercial Sex: The New Slave Trade.* Frank Cass. London.

14. Williams, 1999.

15. Hawkins, D. 2002, *Power vs. Force: The Hidden Determinants of Human Behavior.* Hay House, Carlsbad, California, p. 216.

16. Schwartz, G.J.1999. "Empowerment and Denigration: the ambivalence of femininity in modern Thai society." Paper completed and presented in Hartshorne seminar, University of Wisconsin, Madison Geography department.

17. Skrobanek, S., Bookpakdi, N., and Janthakeero, C., 1997.

18. Transcribed interview from television show "Rediscovering Biology: Molecular to Global Perspectives," on Oregon Public Broadcasting, 30 April 2010.

19. UNICEF Progress for Children Report, 2007.

20. Chrisler, J. within Within Paludi, Michele A. Ed. *Feminism and Women's Rights Worldwide*, Vol. 3. ABC CLIO Press, Santa Barbara.

21. Clawson and Johnson, 2003.

22. UNESCO 2009, The State of the World's Children Report and ILO, A global alliance against forced labor: 2005.

23. "Owed Justice," 2000: 25-26.

24. UN estimates, found in State Department Trafficking in Persons Report, 2003.
25. Bush plan chronology taken from: Troubnikoff, Anna M. Ed., 2003. *Trafficking in Women and Children: Current Issues and Developments,* Nova Publishing, New York.
26. Clinton plan chronology taken from Troubnikoff, 2003.
27. http://www.usinfo.state.gov/gi/Archive/2004/May/12-381449.html, Accessed April 2010.

Other Sources

Austin, J.L., J.O. Urmson and Marina Sbisa, eds., 1975. *How to Do Things with Words*. Cambridge, MA: Harvard University Press.

Bell, David et. al. Eds., 2001. *Pleasure Zones: Bodies, Cities, Spaces.* Syracuse University Press.

Brennan, Denise, 2004. *What's Love Got to Do with it: Transnational Desires and Sex Tourism in the Dominican Republic.* Durham, NC: Duke University Press.

Butler, Judith. 1997. The *Psychic Life of Power: Theories in Subjection.* Stanford University Press.

Foucault, Michel, 1990. *The History of Sexuality, Vol I-III.* Vintage Books, New York.

Hubbard, Phil, 1998, "Sexuality, Immorality and the City: Red-Light Districts and the Marginalization of Female Street Prostitutes." *Gender, Place & Culture: A Journal of Feminist Geography,* 5(1): 55-76.

Ingold, Tim, 1993. "Globes and Spheres: The topology of environmentalism." In Kay Milton, ed. *Environmentalism.* New York: Routledge. 31-42.

Jeffrey, Leslie Ann, 2002. *Sex and Borders: Gender, National Identity, and Prostitution Policy in Thailand.* UBC Press. Vancuver.

Kempadoo, Kamala, and Doezema Jo. Eds., 1998. *Global Sex Workers: Rights, Resistance, and Redefinition.* Routledge, New York.

Laqueur, Thomas Walter, 1992. *Making Sex: Body and Gender from the Greeks to Freud.* Harvard University Press.

Martin, E., 1994. *Flexible Bodies: tracking immunity in American culture from the Days of Polio to the Age of AIDS.* Beacon Press.

Pattanaik, Bandana, and Susanne Thorbek, Eds., 2002. *Transnational Prostitution: changing global patterns.* Zed Books. London, 123.

Seabrook, Jeremy. 2001. *Travels in the Skin Trade: Tourism and the Sex Industry.* Pluto Press. London.

Steady, Filomina Chioma, 2002. *Black Women, Globalization, and Economic Justice: Studies from Africa and the African Diaspora.* Schenkman Books. Rochester, Vermont.

Visweswaran, Kamala, 1994. *Fictions of Feminist Ethnography.* University of Minnesota Press.

White, Luise, 1994. The *Comforts of Home: Prostitution in Colonial Nairobi.* University of Chicago Press.

Our Exploding Population

1. Concept taken from Gore, A. 2005, "An Inconvenient Truth" documentary film.

2. www.worldatlas.com, Accessed February 2010.
3. www.overpopulation.org, Accessed February 2010.
4. World Population Data Sheet 2009 and www.oxfam.com
5. McGovern, G. 2001. "The Real Cost of Hunger," Accessed June 2010 from http://www.thefreelibrary.com/The+real+cost+of+hunger-a086062268
6. Kiesel, L. 2009. "Why is the Media Afraid to Tackle Livestock's Role in Climate Change?" November 3, www.solveclimate.com, Accessed in February 2010.
7. Christopherson, R., 2010. *Elemental Ecosystems*, Pearson Prentice-Hall, New Jersey, pg. 542.
8. UN Food and Agriculture Organization Report, 2008.

The So-Called Drug War

1. Harman, Danna, 2005. Christian Science Monitor, August 16, "Mexicans take over drug trade to U.S: With Colombian cartels in shambles, Mexican drug lords run the show."
2. Bulmer-Thomas, Victor, and James Dunkerley, Eds., 1999. *The United States and Latin America: The New Agenda.* Institute of Latin American Studies at University of London.
3. Gerber, Jurg, and Eric L. Jensen, Ed., 2001. *Drug War American Style.* Garland. New York.
4. Bulmer-Thomas, 1999: 162.
5. Amnesty International 1990: 70.
6. Huggins, M.K. 1991. "Vigilantism and the State in Modern Latin America," in M.K. Huggins Ed., *U.S. Supported State Terror – A History of Police Training in Latin America* (pp. 219-242) Praeger. New York.
7. Gerber, 2001: 182
8. www.whitehousedrugpolicy.gov, Accessed September 2006.
9. Schweich, Thomas, 2008. New York Times "Is Afghanistan a Narco-state?" July 27.

10. Schweich, Thomas, 2008.
11. Schweich, Thomas, 2008.
12. Astorga, Luis, UNESCO discussion paper no. 36, "Drug Trafficking in Mexico: A first General Assessment."
13. Rashid, Ahmed, 2008. *Descent into Chaos: The United States, and the Failure of Nation Building in Pakistan, Afghanistan, and Central Asia.* Penguin Books, New York.
14. Dreyfuss, Robert, 2005. *Devil's Game: How the United States Helped Unleash Fundamentalist Islam.* New York, NY. Metropolitan Books, pg. 326.
15. Schweich, Thomas, 2008.
16. www.colombiasupport.net, Accessed October 2007.

Other Sources

Allen, Christian M. 2005. *An Industrial Geography of Cocaine.* Routledge.

Bagley, Bruce M., and William O. Walker III, Eds., 1994. *Drug trafficking in the Americas. Transaction Publishers.*

Joyce, Elizabeth and Carlos Melanuel, Eds. 1988. *Latin America and the Multi-national Drug Trade.* MacMillan Press.

Mabry, Donald J. Ed., 1989. *The Latin American Narcotics Trade and US National Security.* Greenwood Press. Westport, CT.

MacDonald, Scott B. 1988. *Dancing on a Volcano.* Praeger.

Morales, Edmundo, 1989. *Cocaine: White Gold Rush in Peru.* University of Arizona Press.

Murillo, Mario A. 2004. *Colombia and the United States: War, Unrest, and Destabilization.* Seven Stories Press. New York.

Vellinga, Menno, Ed., 2004. *The Political Economy of the Drug Industry: Latin America and the International System.* University Press of Florida, Gainsville.

Zirnite, P. 1998. "The Militarization of the Drug War in Latin America." *Current History* 97: 166-173.

Dependence on Oil

1. Pilger, John, 2002. *The New Rulers of the World.* Verso,London and New York.
2. Pilger, 2002.
3. Vidal, Gore, 2003. *Dreaming War: Blood for Oil and the Cheney/Bush Junta.* Nation Books. New York, 13.
4. Leech, Garry., 2006. *Crude Interventions: The United States, Oil, and the New Global (Dis)Order.* Zed Books. London and New York, 29.
5. Leech, 2006: 32.
6. Leech, 2006: 36.
7. "Alaska's Last Oil," National Georaphic Channel, November 2009.
8. "Alaska's Last Oil," National Georaphic Channel, November 2009.
9. Gelbspan, Ross., 2004. *Boiling Point: How Politicians, Big Oil and Coal, Journalists, and Activists are Fueling the Climate Crisis – and What we can do to Avert Disaster.* Basic Books. New York.
10. Gelbspan, 2004.
11. Bykoff, Maxwell T. and Jules M., 2004. "Balance as Bias: Global Warming and the U.S. Prestige Press." *Global Environmental Change* (14), 125-136.
12. Harper's Index 2003.
13. Gelbspan, 2004: 51.
14. Klare, Michael T., 2004. *Blood and Oil: the dangers and consequences of America's Growing Dependency.* Henry Hold and Company, 59.

15. Gelbspan, 2004: 70, 72.
16. Gelbspan, 2004: 69.
17. http://www.itopf.com/information-services/data-and-statistics/statistics/#no, Accessed May   2006.
18. http://envirowonk.com/content/view/68/1/, Accessed May 2006.

Other Sources

Everest, Larry, 2004. *Oil Power, and Empire: Iraq and the US Global Agenda.* Common Courage Press.

Klare, Michael T., 2001. *Resource Wars: the New Landscape of Global Conflict.* Henry Holt and Company. New York.

Miller, David Ed., 2004. *Tell Me Lies: propaganda and media distortion in the attack on Iraq. Pluto Press.*

Miniter, Richard, 2004. *Shadow War: the Untold Story of How Bush is Winning the War on Terror.* Regenery Publishing, Inc. Washington, D.C.

Pelletiere, Stephen, 2004. *America's Oil Wars.* Praeger.

Scott, Peter Dale, 2003. *Drugs, Oil, and War.* Rowan & Littlefield.

Sperry, Paul, 2003. *Crude Politics.* WND Books.

Yetiv, Steve A., 2004. *Crude Awakenings: Global Oil Security and American Foreign Policy.* Cornell University Press.

A Rising Tide Lifts All Boats

1. United Nations Publications, 2006. "In-Depth Study on All Forms of Violence against Women" Report of the Secretary General. A/61/122/Add.1. 6 July.

2. *World Bank Study World Development Report,* 1993 "Investing in Health", New York, Oxford University Press.

Solar Energy

1. http://www.cnbc.com/id/17483073/Ted_Turner_Touts_ Solar_Power_And_Invests_In_It, Accessed November, 2009.
2. Butler, Declan, 2007."Solar Power: California's latest gold rush." Nature, 450 (6).
3. U.S. Energy Information Administration: http://www.eia. doe.gov/oiaf/ieo/highlights.html, Accessed July 2010.
4. Kryza, Frank, 2003. *The Power of Light: The Epic Story of Man's Quest to Harness the Sun.* McGraw-Hill, XIII
5. Kryza, Frank, 2003.
6. Kryza, Frank, 2003.
7. "Solar Power to the Masses," Institute of Science in Society Report July 31, 2008.
8. "Solar Power to the Masses," Institute of Science in Society Report July 31, 2008.
9. Goetzberger, A. and V.U. Hoffmann, 2005. *Photovoltaic Solar Energy Generation.* Springer, Heidelberg.
10. Carless, Jennifer, 1993. *Renewable Energy: a Concise Guide to Green Alternatives.* Walker and Company, New York.
11. http://www.businessgreen.com/business-green/ news/2259302/sunedison-eyeing-plans-world, Accessed June 2010.
12. http://www.businessgreen.com/business-green/ news/2259302/sunedison-eyeing-plans-world, Accessed May 2010.
13. Carless, 1993.
14. http://apps1.eere.energy.gov/news/news_detail.cfm/news_ id=11490, Accessed June 2010.
15. Bradford, Travis, 2006. *Solar Revolution: the Economic Transformation of the Global Energy Industry.* MIT Press.

16. Butler, Declan, 2007.
17. Bradford, 2006.
18. Freeman, David S. 2007. *Wining Our Energy Independence: An energy insider shows how.* Gibbs Smith, Salt Lake City.
19. http://www.msnbc.msn.com/id/16577883/, Accessed May 2010.
20. Singh, Madanjeet, 1998. *The Timeless Energy of the Sun for Life and Peace with Nature.* Unesco Publishing.
21. http://en.wikipedia.org/wiki/World_energy_resources_and_ consumption, Accessed July 2010.
22. Dickerson, Marla, 2010. "Tokyo's goal: Be the greenest." Los Angeles Times, April 23.
23. Carless, 1993.
24. "The Greenhouse Effect," Greenpeace Publications, 2000, 2-3.
25. Bradford, T. and Katzman, M., 2006. *Solar and Wind Energy: An Economic Evaluation of Current and Future Technologies.* Rowman and Littlefield.
26. Bradford, 2006.
27. Bradford, T. and Katzman, M. 2006.
28. http://www.cnbc.com/id/17483073/Ted_Turner_Touts_ Solar_Power_And_Invests_In_It. Accessed May 2010.
29. Bradford, 2006.

Other Sources

Beattie, Donald A. Ed., 1997. *History and Overview of the Solar Heat Technologies.* MIT Press Cambridge and London.

Fanchi, John R., 2005. *Energy in the 21st Century.* World Scientific Publishing.

Halacy, D.S. Jr., 1973. *The Coming Age of Solar Energy.* Harper and Row Publishers. New York.

Knight, Matthew, 2010. "A Dazzling Future for Solar Power?" May 12, CNN.com

Miyake, Jun, Yasuo Igarashi, and Matthias Rogner, Eds., 2004. *Biohydrogen III, Renewable Energy Systems by Biological Solar Energy Converstion.* Elsevier. Oxford.

Renewables Information: 2006. International Energy Agency. OECD/IEA.

Stanley, Tom, 2004. *Going Solar: Understanding and Using the Warmth in Sunlight.* Stonefield Pubulishing.

Benevolent Individuals

1. *Time* Magazine, May 10, 2010. "The 100 Most Influential People in the World."
2. Gaudiani, Claire, 2003. *The Greater Good: How Philanthropy Drives the American Economy and Can Save Capitalism.* Times Books.
3. Fleishman, Joel L. 2007. "Philanthropic Leadership: A Personal Perspective." Presentation to HSBC Bank, USA. Accessed May 2007 from http://us.hsbc.com/privatebanking/wealth/pb_fleishman.asp.
4. Gaudiani, 2003: 2.
5. Gaudiani, 2003.
6. *Time* Magazine, May 10, 2010. "The 100 Most Influential People in the World."
7. Auletta, Ken, 2004. *Media Man: Ted Turner's Improbable Empire.* Atlas Books, 30.
8. Auletta, 2004.
9. Auletta, 2004.
10. http://www.turnerfoundation.org, Accessed November 2006.
11. http://www.renewableenergyworld.com/rea/news/article/2010/03/southern-company-ted-turner-acquire-first-solar-project, Accessed July 2010.

12. Gaudiani, 2003: 17
13. http://www.oprah.com, Accessed December 2006.
14. http://www.learningtogive.org, Accessed January 2007.

Other Sources

Adam, Thomas, Ed., 2004. *Philanthropy, Patronage, and Civil Society: Experiences from Germany, Great Britain, and North America.* Indiana University Press.

Anheier, Helmut and Diana Leat, Eds., 2006. *Creative Philanthropy: toward a new philanthropy for the 21st century.* Routledge Press.

Bonner, Michael, Mine Ener, Amy Singer, Eds., 2003. *Poverty and Charity in Middle Eastern Contexts.* State University of New York Press.

Clift, Elayne, Ed., 2005. *Women, Philanthropy, and Social Change: Vision for a just society.* Tufts University Press.

De Borms, Luc Tayart, 2005. *Foundations: Creating Impact in a Globalised World.* John Wiley & Sons, Ltd.

Gasman, Marybeth and Katherine V. Sedgwick Eds., 2005. *Uplifting a People.* Peter Lang.

Gregory, Robert G., 1992. *The Ride and Fall of Philanthropy in East Africa: The Asian Contribution.* Transaction Publishers.

Hopkins, Elwood M., 2005. *Collaborative Philanthropies: What Groups of Foundations Can Do that Individual Funders Cannot.* Lexington Books, Boulder.

Nagel, Stuart S Ed., 1994. *Eastern European Development and Public Policy.* St. Martin's Press.

Oliner, Samuel P. 2003. *Do Unto Others: Extraordinary Acts of Ordinary People*. Westview Press.

http://news.target.com/phoenix.zhtml?c=196187&p=irol-newsarticle&ID=932586, Accessed June 2007.

Organic Agriculture

1. Garcia, Deborah Koons, 2001. "The Future of Food." Motion Picture.
2. Duram, Leslie A., 2005.Good Growing: Why Organic Farming Works. University of Nebraska Press, Lincoln and London.
3. Kuepper, George, and Lange Cegner, 2004. *Organic Crop Production Overview*. National Sustainable Agriculture Information Service. August.
4. Berry, Wendell, 1977. *The Unsettling of America: Culture and Agriculture*. San Francisco. Sierra Club Books. From Duram, Leslie A., 2005.
5. Duram, 1994.
6. Magdoff, F., JB Foster, and F. Buttel Eds., 2000. *Hungry for Profit: The Agribusiness Threat to Farmers, Food, and the Environment*. New York: Monthly Reviews Press.
7. Jaffe, Gregory A., 2001. *Lessen the Fear of Genetically Engineered Crops*. Christian Science Monitor, August 8, pg. 8.
8. Magdoff, 2000.
9. Taken from documentary motion picture "Food, Inc."
10. Swanby, H. and Wilson, S., 2005. "Smoke screen or solution? Genetic engineering and food   insecurity," within Wilson, Shamillah, Anasuya Sengupta, and Kristy Evans, Eds. *Defending Our Dreams: Global feminist voices for a new generation.* Zed Books, London.
11. Tewolde, B., 2001, "The Use of Genetically Modified Crops in Agriculture and Food Production and Their Impacts on the Environment – a Developing World

Perspective." Ethiopia: Ethiopian Environmental Protection
Authority, p. 1.

12. Peter, D. and Ghesquiere, P. Bilan, 1988. *des connaissances
et des applications de l'agriculture biologique et interet
pour l'agriculture Communautaire.* Commission of the
European Communities, Brussels.

13. Lampkin, N.H. and S. Padel, Eds., 1994. *The Economics
of Organic Farming: An International Perspective.* Cab
International, Wallingford.

14. Thompson, 2000.

15. "Organic Agriculture and Rural Poverty Alleviation." 2002.
Economic and Social Commission for Asia and the Pacific
Potential and Best Practices in Asia. United Nations.
New York.

16. *Eco-Farming: The Chinese Experience.* 2000. Published
through the United Nations Environment Program (UNEP).

17. http://www.search.ers.USDA.gov, Accessed January 2007.

18. Worthington, Virginia, 2001. "Effect of Agricultural
Methods on Nutritional Quality: A comparison of Organic
with Conventional Crops": *Alternative Therapies,* 1998.
4(1):58-69. AND Worthington, Virginia. "Nutritional
Quality of Organic Versus Conventional Fruits, Vegetables,
and Grains." *Journal of Alternative and Complimentary
Medicine.* 7(2): 161-173.

19. Byrum, Allison. "Organically Grown Foods Higher
in Cancer-Fighting Chemicals than Conventionally
Grown Foods." American Chemical Society Public
ReleaseAccessed March 2003 from http://www.eurekalert.
org/pub_pubreleases/2003-03/acs-ogfo30303.php.

20. Grinder, 2003.

21. Duram, 2003: 5.

22. Heaton, Shane, 2001. "Organic Farming, Food Quality,
and Human Health Report. Briefing Sheet." UK Soil
Association. http://www.soilassociation.org/web/sa/saweb.
nsf.librarytitoles/briefing_sheets03-8200a, Accessed
November 2005.

23. Heaton, 2001.
24. OECD Working Papers, 2000. "Comparing the Profitability of Organic and Conventional Farming: The Impact of Support on Arable Farming in France."
25. Faeth, P., R. Repetto, K. Kroll, Q. Dai, and G. Helmers, 1991. *Paying the Farm Bill: U.S. Agricultural Policy and the Transition to Sustainable Agriculture*. World Resources Institute, Washington, D.C.

Other Sources

Curl, Cynthia L. Richard A Fenske, and Kai Elgethun 2003. "Organi-phosphorous Pesticide Exposure of Urban and Suburban Preschool Children with Organic and Conventional Diets." *Environmental Health Perspectives* 111 (3): 377-382

Dimitri, Carolyn and Catherine Green. 2002. "Recent Growth Patterns in the US Organic Foods Market." *USDA Economic Research Service, Agriculture Information Bulletin no. 777.*

Green, Catherine, and Amy Kremen. 2003. "US Organic Farming in 2000-2002: Adoption of Certified Systems." *USDA Economic Research Service, Agriculture Information Bulletin no. 780.*

"Organic Food and Beverages: World Supply and Major European Markets." 1999. International Trade Centre, Geneva.

Pedersen, Lisbeth, S. Rasmussen, S. Bugel, L. Jargensen, L. Dragsted, V. Gundersen, and B. Sandstrom, 2003. "Effects of Diets Based on Foods from Conventional Versus Organic Production and Intake and Excretion of Flavinoids and Markers of Defence in Humans." *Journal of Agricultural and Good Chemistry*. 51 (19): 5671-76.

Pesticide Action Network of North America, 2003.

Wilson, Shamillah, Anasuya Sengupta, and Kristy Evans, Eds., 2005. *Defending Our Dreams: Global feminist voices for a new generation.* Zed Books, London.

"World Markets for Organic Fruit and Vegetables: Opportunities for developing countries in the production and export of organic horticultural products." 2001. International Trade Centre, Technical Centre for the Agricultural and Rural Cooperation. Food and Agriculture Organization of the United Nations. Rome.

Worldwatch Paper 73. 1986. "Beyond the Green Revolution: New approaches for Third World Agriculture." October.

http://www.wikipedia.org/wiki/organoponicos, Accessed February 2007.

Benevolent Organizations

1. Union of International Association, 2004.
2. http://nobelprize.org, Accessed October, 2006.
3. Miechel, Robert Cameron, 1985. "From Conservation to the Environmental Movement." *Resources for the Future.* Washington, D.C: 2.
4. Rodrigues, Maria Guadalupe Moog, 2004. *Global Environmentalism and Local Politics: Transnational Advocacy Networks in Brazil, Ecuador and India.* State University of New York Press.
5. *200 NG0s in China: A Special Report from the China Development Brief.* January, 2005.
6. McKinley, E.H. 1995. *Marching to Glory: The History of The Salvation Army in the United States, 1880-1992.* (Ch. 6) Williams B. Eerdmands Publishing Company. Cambridge and Grand Rapids.

7. Richmond, Oliver P. Ed., 2005. And Henry F. Carey. *Subcontracting Peace: The Challenges of NGO Peacebuilding.* Ashgate.
8. 200 NGOs in China, 2005.
9. www.clintonglobalinitiative.org/aboutus accessed May 2010.
10. Interview on The Daily Show with Jon Stewart, aired September 17, 2009.
11. Eversole, Robyn Ed., 2003 *Here to Help: NGOs Combating Poverty in Latin America.* M.E. Sharpe. New York and London.
12. Swarts, Frederick A, 2003. "NGOs and Environmental Conservation." From Hamad, Tajeldin, et al. *Culture of Responsibility and the Role of NGOs.* Continuum International Publishing Group.
13. 200 NGOs in China, 2005.
14. "NGOs in Consultative Status with ECOSOC" Department of Economic and Social Affairs. http://ww.un.org/esa/coordination/ngo/about.html, Accessed June 2005.
15. Richmond, 2005.
16. Gunter, Michael M. Jr. *Building the Next Ark: How NGOs Work to Protect Biodiversity.* Dartmouth College Press, 2004.
17. Hamad, Tajeldin, Frederick Swarts, and Anne Ranniste Smart, Eds., 2003. *Culture of Responsibility and the Role of NGOs.* Continuum International Publishing Group.
18. http://www.forbes.com/2003/10/23/cx_aw_1023giving.html, Accessed July 2010.
19. Hopgood, Stephen, 2006. *Keepers of the Flame: Understanding Amnesty International.* Cornell University Press.
20. Hopgood, 2006.

Other Sources

Bryant, Raymond L., 2005. *Nongovernmental Organizations in Environmental Struggles: Politics and the Making of Moral Capital in the Philippines.* Yale University Press.

Heere, Wybo P. Ed., 2004. *From Government to Governance: The Growing Impact of Non-state Actors in the International and European Legal System.* TMC Asser Press. The Hague.

Keck, Margaret E. and Kathryn Sikkink, 1998. *Activists Beyond Borders: Advocacy Networks in International Politics.* Cornell University Press. Ithaca, NY.

Martens, Kerstin, 2005. *NGOs and the United Nations: Institutionalization, Professionalization, and Adaptation.* Palgrave-McMillan. New York.

McCloskey, J. Michael, 2005. *In the Thick of It: My Life in the Sierra Club.* Island Press. Washington.

Minnear, Larry and Weiss, Thomas, 1995. *Mercy Under Fire: War and the Global Humanitarian Community.* Westview. Boulder, CO.

Pease, Kelly-Kate S., 2000. *International Organizations: Perspectives on Governance in the Twenty-First Century.* Prentice Hall. New Jersey.

Raven, Peter H., 1990. "AIBS News: The Politics of Preserving Biodiversity." *Bioscience* 40, No. 10. November, 771.

Ticknet, Joel, Carolyn Rafensperger, and Nancy Myers, "The Precautionary Principle in Action: A Handbook First Edition." Science and Environmental Health Network. Accessed May 2003 from http://www,biotech-info.net/precautionary.html.

Willets, Peter, Ed., 1996. *The Conscience of the World: The Influence of Non-Governmental Organizations in the UN System.* Hurst. London.

The Rise of Women

1. As quoted from appearance on "The Oprah Winfrey Show,"April 13, 2010
2. Momsen, Janet Henshall, 1991. *Women and Development in the Third World.* Routledge, London.
3. Momsen, 1991.
4. http://teacher.scholastic.com/activities/suffrage/history/htm. Accessed June 2010.
5. http://www.globalfundforwomen.org accessed June 2010.
6. *World Bank Study World Development Report,* 1993 "Investing in Health", New York, Oxford University Press.
7. Momsen, 1991.
8. FAO, 2002 "Gender and Food Security," accessed from http://www.fao.org/gender/en/agri-e.htm>.
9. Paludi M., Martin J., Paludi C., Boggess S., Hicks K., Speech L., 2010. "Pay Equity as justice: United States and International Perspectives." Within Paludi, Michele A. Ed. *Feminism and Women's Rights Worldwide*, Vol. 3. ABC CLIO Press, Santa Barbara.
10. Paludi, et. al. within Paludi, M. 2010.
11. Momsen, 1991.
12. Momsen, 1991.
13. United Nations Population Fund Activities Report, 2005.
14. UNICEF, 2007.
15. UNICEF, 2007.
16. Charles M. and Bradley K. 2002, "Equal but Separate: A cross-national study of sex segregation in higher education." *American Sociological Review*, 67, 573-599.
17. UN Population Fund Activities Report, 2005.

18. Charles and Bradley, 2002.
19. Sharma, Om Parkash and Robert D. Tetherford, 1990. *Effect of Female Literacy on Fertility in India.* New Delhi: Office of the Registrar General & Census Commissioner, and Ministry of Home Affairs, Government of India, pg. 27.
20. Sharma, 1990.
21. Basow, Susan, "Women in Education: Students and Professors Worldwide" within Paludi, Michele A. Ed. 2010. Vol 1.
22. Sharma, 1990.
23. Basow within Paludi, 2010, vol. 1.
24. Sen, Gita, Adrienne Germain, and Lincoln C. Chen, 1994. *Population Policies Reconsidered: Health, Empowerment, and Rights.* Harvard University Press.
25. Dreze, J.P., and A.K. Sen, 1989. *Hunger and Public Action.* Oxford: Clarendon Press.
26. Sen and Chen, 1994.
27. Brizendine, L. 2006. "The Female Brain," Broadway Books, New York.
28. Haddad E., and Schweinle W. "The Feminine Political Persona: Queen Victoria, Ellen Johnson Sirleaf, and Michelle Bachelet." Within Paludi, 2010, vol. 1.
29. Eagley and Carli, 2007. *Through the Labyrinth.* Boston: Harvard Business School Press.
30. Eagley, A.H. and Hohanneson-Schmidt, M.C. 2001, "The Leadership Styles of Women and Men." *Journal of Social Issues*, 57, 781-797 and Walumba, Wi, and Ojode, 2004, "Gender and Instructional Outcomes: The mediating role of leadership style." *Journal of Management Development*, 23, 124-140, Within Haddad, et. al. 2010.
31. Eagley and Hohanneson-Schmidt, 2001, and Walumba and Ojode, 2004.
32. Haddad within Paludi, Michele A, 2010. Vol.1, pg. 98.
33. Sen, Gita, Adrienne Germain, and Lincoln C. Chen, 1994, pg. 71.

34. Hamad, Tajeldin, Frederick Swarts, and Anne Ranniste Smart, Eds., 2003. *Culture of Responsibility and the Role of NGOs.* Continuum International Publishing Group.
35. Blumberg, Rae Lesser, et al. Eds., 1995. *EnGENDERing Wealth and Well-Being: Empowerment for Global Change.* Westview Press, Boulder.
36. Blumberg, 1995.
37. UNICEF: Progress for Children Report, 2007.
38. UNICEF: Progress for Children Report, 2007.
39. Diop-Sidibe, Campbell, & Becker, 2005, "Domestic Violence Against Women in Egypt: Wife beating and health outcomes." Social Science & Medicine, 62, 1260-1277 and Chrisler, Joan and Cynthia Garrett, "Women's Reproductive Rights: An International Perspective." Within Paludi, 2010, vol. 3.
40. Pettifor, Measham, Reef, & Padian, 2004, "Sexual Power and HIV Risk, South Africa. Emerging Infectious Diseases." Accessed May 2010 from http://www.cdc.gov/ncidod/EID/vol10no11/04-0252.htm.
41. UNICEF: Progress for Children, 2005.
42. Steinem, Gloria, 2010. "A child bride, fighting for her rights," *Time* magazine, May 10, pg. 148.
43. Ahmed, Aziza, 2005. "Chanelling Discourse, Effecting Change: young women and sexual rights." Within Wilson, Shamillah, Anasuya Sengupta, and Kristy Evans, Eds. *Defending Our Dreams: Global feminist voices for a new generation.* Zed Books, London.
44. "More Catholic bishops deny communion to pro-choice politicians." October 2004, *Church & State*, p. 19-20.
45. Butt, R. 2009, "Condom use could make HIV/AIDS situation worse in Africa, says Pope: controversy over Catholic church's stance reignited – Policy divides some clergy working with patients." *Guardian,* p. 18.
46. UNICEF: Progress for Children, 2007.
47. UNICEF, 2007 pg. 30 and UNICEF 2009, The State of the

World's Children Report, Table 4: HIV/AIDS and Table 8: Women.

48. UNICEF, 2007, pg. 33.
49. S. Correa, 1996. "From reproductive health to sexual rights: achievements and future   challenges." From Ahmed, 2005.
50. Garcia-Moreno, c. Jansen, H.A.F.M., Ellseberg, M., Heise, L.L. and watts, C.H. 2005, WHO multi-country study on women's health and domestic violence against women: initial results on prevalence, health outcomes and women's responses. Switzerland: World health Organization.
51. Stiglmayer, A. 1993, "A pattern of rape: A torrent of wrenching first-person testimonies tells of a now Serb atrocity: Systematic sexual abuse." *Newsweek.* Accessed May 2010 at http://www.newsweek.com/id/115892.
52. Swiss, S. & Giller, J. 1993, "Rape as a crime of war: A medical perspective." *Journal of the American Medical Association,* 270, 612-615.
53. Amnesty International, 2004. "Lives blown apart: crimes against women in armed conflict." London: Amnesty International Publications. Accessed May 2010 from http://www.amnesty.org/en/library/info/ACT77/075/2004.
54. Mithers, C. 2004, "The garden of evil." Accessed May 2010 from http://www.globalfundforwomen.org/cms/press-center/2004-gfw-news/garden-of-evil.html
55. Mithers, 2004.
56. UNICEF, 2007.
57. UNICEF, 2007.
58. Sen, 1994, pg. 143.
59. Blumberg, 1995, pg. 155.

Other Sources

Domosh, Mona and Joni Seager, 2001. *Putting Women in Place.* New York: Guilford Press.

Duran, Lydia A., Noel D. Payne, and Anahi Russo, Eds., 2007. *Building Feminist Movements and Organizations: Global Perspectives*. Zed Books, London.

Elias, Marlene and Judith Carney., 2005. "Shea Butter, Globalization, and the Women of Burkina Faso." In Lise Nelson and Joni Seager, eds., *A Companion to Feminist Geography*. Malden, MA: Blackwell Publishing. 93-108.

Erler, Mary C. and Maryanne Kowaleski, Eds., 2003. *Gendering the Master Narrative: Women and Power in the Middle Ages*, Cornell University Press, Ithaca.

Fraser, Arvonne S., and Irene Tinker, Eds., 2004. Developing Power: How Women Transformed International Development. The Feminist Press at The City University of New York. New York.

Haraway, Donna, 1991. *Simians, Cyborgs, and Women*. London: Free Association Books. 127-148.

Harding, Sandra, ed., 2004. *The Feminist Standpoint Theory Reader*. New York: Routledge.

Hooks, Bell, 2000. *Feminism is for Everybody: Passionate Politics*. Cambridge, MA: Southend Press.

Massey, Doreen, 1994. *Space, Place and Gender,* Minneapolis: University of Minnesota.

McGuire , Judy, and Barry Popkin, 1990. "Helping Women Improve Nutrition in the Developing World: Beating the Zero-Sum Game," World Bank technical Paper, no. 114 (Washington, DC: WorldBank.

Medrano, Diana, and Rodrigo Villar, 1988. *Mujer campasina y organizacion rural en Colombia: Tres estudios de caso*, Press of Universidad de los Andes (CEREC).

Paludi, Michele A. Ed., 2010. *Feminism and Women's Rights Worldwide Vol. 1,2,3*. ABC CLIO Press, Santa Barbara.

Parpart, Jane L., Shirin M. Rai, and Kathleen Staudt, Eds., 2002. *Rethinking Empowerment: Gender and development in a global/local world*. Routledge, London.

Sangari, Kumkum, and Uma Chakravarti, Eds., 1999. *From Myths to Markets: Essays on Gender*. Manohar Publishers, New Delhi.

Viswanath, Vanita, 1991. *NGOs and Women's Develoment in Rural South India: A Comparative Analysis*. Westview Press, Boulder.

Wilson, Shamillah, Anasuya Sengupta, and Kristy Evans, Eds., 2005. *Defending Our Dreams: Global feminist voices for a new generation*. Zed Books, London.

Living More Efficiently

1. Rodgers, Heather, 2005. *The Hidden Life of Garbage*, The New Press.
2. http://www.bread.org/hunger/global/, Accessed on July 2010.
3. Hellmich, N., 2010, "U.S. obesity rate leveling off, at about one-third of adults." *USA Today* 1/13/2010. Accessed in June 2010 from: http://www.usatoday.com/news/health/weightloss/2010-01-13-obesity-rates_N.htm
4. McCandless, D. "Information is beautiful," *Above Magazine: for the Earth*. Spring 2010, UK.
5. Federal Trade Commission statistics, Accessed in July 2010 from http://www.ftc.gov/opa/2003/06/2001cigrpt.shtm

6. McGovern, G. 2001. "The Real Cost of Hunger," Accessed June 2010 from http://www.thefreelibrary.com/ The+real+cost+of+hunger-a086062268

7. http://www.thirdworldtraveler.com/Global_Secrets_Lies/ Myth_FoodScarcity.html, Accessed June 2010.

8. http://www.thirdworldtraveler.com/Global_Secrets_Lies/ Myth_FoodScarcity.html, Accessed June 2010.

9. McGovern, G., 2001 "The Real Cost of Hunger,"

10. Aumaitre,A.L and J.G. Boyazoglu, 2010, "A note on livestock production and consumption   in Europe." European Association for Animal Production, Via Nomentana 134, Rome 00162 Italy

11. Wikipedia.org, accessed July 2010

12. Shah, A. 2010. "Beef," March 21, Accessed June 2010 from http://www.globalissues.org/article/240/beef

13. Shah, A. 2010.

14. http://www.thirdworldtraveler.com/Global_Secrets_Lies/ Myth_FoodScarcity.html, Accessed June 2010.

15. Gabler R., Petersen J., and Trapasso L. 2007. *Essentials of Physical Geography*, 8th Ed. Thomson Brooks/Cole. Belmont, California.

16. Vandana Shiva, 2000, *Stolen Harvest*, South End Press, pp. 70-71.

17. Shah, A. 2010.

18. UN Development Program – Human Development Report 2006. Accessed in May, 2010 from: http://www.data360. org/dsg.aspx?Data_Set_Group_Id=757

19. Schwartz, G. 1998 "Las Vegas, Baby: escaping reality and glimpsing the future in America's most infamous city." MS thesis, University of Wisconsin, Madison, Geography Dept.

20. http://www.water-ed.org/watersources/community. asp?rid=8&cid=524, Accessed May 2010.

21. http://ca.water.usgs.gov/groundwater/gwatlas/valley/ landsub.html, Accessed June 2010

22. http://ca.water.usgs.gov/groundwater/gwatlas/valley/ landsub.html, Accessed June 2010

23. http://www.globalchange.umich.edu/globalchange2/current/ lectures/freshwater supply/freshwater.html, Accessed June 2010.
24. Los Angeles Department of Water and Power, home mailer, February 2010.
25. http://www.aph.gov.au/library/pubs/rn/2006-07/07rn12.pdf, accessed July 2010.
26. Taken from documentary film "Who Killed the Electric Car?" 2006.
27. "Who Killed the Electric Car?" 2006.
28. Costanza, B., 2001 "GM sues California's smog board." CBSmarketwatch.com, 24 Feb. Accessed June 2010.
29. http://www.hybridcenter.org/hybrid-vs-hummer.html, Accessed July 2010.
30. http://www.hybridcenter.org/hybrid-vs-hummer.html, Accessed July 2010.
31. Curlee, T. Randal. Schexnayder, Vogt, Wolfe, Kelsay, and Feldman, 1994. *Waste to Energy in the United States: A social and economic assessment.* Quorum Books: 2.
32. Kreith, Frank, Ed., 1994. *Handbook of Solid Waste Management.* McGraaw-Hill.
33. Sayers, Dorothy L., 1942. "Why Work?"
34. http://www.tufts.edu/tuftsrecycles/USstates.htm, Accessed October, 2008.
35. http://hopebuilding.pbworks.com/Biogas-plants-in-Rwandan-prisons-treat-sewage,-generate-biogas-and-crop-fertilizer,-and-save-trees, Accessed July 2010.
36. California IWMB. "Last Chance Mercantile: A model for local government recycling and waste reduction. 2002": 1.
37. Dickerson, M., 2010. "Tokyo's goal: Be the greenest." *Los Angeles Times*, April 23.
38. Dickerson, M., 2010.
39. *Biocycle Magazine* Annual Survey, 2004.
40. California Integrated Waste Management Board "Organics Options: opportunities for local government reuse, recycling, and composting. 2002": 1.

41. http://www.calrecycle.ca.gov/LGCentral/Library/ innovations/ recoverypark/CaseStudies1.htm, Accessed July 2010.
42. California IWMB. "Taking Packaging for Granted: Can you afford to? 2007": 2.

Other Sources

California Integrated Waste Management Board. "Feasibility Study on the Expanded Use of Agricultural and Forest Waste in Commercial Product. January 1999."

U.S. EPA, 1989. "The Solid Waste Dilemma: An Agenda for Action." Office of Solid Waste and Emergency Response. EPA/530-SW-89-019, February.

Yen, T.F. Ed., 1974. *Recycling and Disposal of Solid Wastes: Industrial, agricultural, domestic.* Ann Arbor Science Publishers.

The Gift of Tragedy

1. Quotation by Osama Bin Laden. "Verbatim," *Time* Magazine, February 8, 2010, pg. 15.
2. http://pages.prodigy.net/unohu/brainwaves.htm#Alpha, accessed September 14, 2010.

Practical Suggestions for Taking Action

1. Fishman, C, 2006, "How Many Light Bulbs Does it Take to Change the World? One, and You're Looking at It" Fast Company Magazine, September 1. Viewed on Sept 29, 2010 at www.fastcompany.com/magazine/108/open_ lightbulbs.html